MSG Denise :

Never Forget! Thank you
For being a First responder.

Ron Arlandagel
11-13-21

i

Command and Control

Command and Control

••

A true story with real people and real events leading up to the September 11, 2001 terrorist attack. The New York Army National Guard was called to duty on September 11, 2001 by the governor of New York, Governor George E. Pataki. Some 1,500 New York City-based National Guard troops immediately reported for state active duty on the morning of 9/11 and another 1,500 from points throughout upstate New York arrived in lower Manhattan by that evening. At the helm in command and control was Headquarters of the 53rd Troop Command. This was the deadliest attacks recorded on U.S. soil in American history. We can never forget the 2,997 souls that lost their lives. You will hear from first responder soldiers describing their call to duty on that horrific day.

Ron Sardanopoli

A certificate of registration was issued by the United States Copywrite Office.

Under the seal of Copywrite office in accordance with title 17, United States Code.

This certificate attests that the registration has been made for the following work

Title: Command and Control. Author Ron Sardanopoli

Registration Number: TXu 2-268-590 Registration decision Date: July 22, 2021

ISBN 9798547767043

Newlands, (Ed)

This book is dedicated to families that lost loved ones during the 9-11 terrorist attack. A tribute of remembrance to those who died, 2,997 souls. That includes 343 firefighters, 23 New York City police officers, 37 Port Authority officers and 55 military personnel. The sacrifice of rescue, recovery, and relief workers. Including those rescue workers who were sickened, or died after responding to the September 11 attacks.

*   *   *

Table of Contents

Preface

Most people typically think of police officers and firefighters when the mentioning of first responders who rushed to the scene at ground zero on September 11, 2001. There was another organization of first responders that charged to ground zero, and made a major impact on the rescue and recovery mission. This organization was the New York Army National Guard-NYARNG. The NYARNG was called to duty on September 11, 2001 by the governor of New York at the time, Governor George E. Pataki. The Governor called to protect and defend our nation following the attack in New York city. Some 1,500 New York City-based National Guard troops immediately reported for state active duty on the morning of 9/11 and another 1,500 from points throughout upstate New York arrived in lower Manhattan by that evening. The Headquarters that received the official order to be in command and control on this horrific day was Headquarters 53rd Troop Command, commanded by Brigadier General Edward G. Klein. I was one of those first responders on duty that day working as a logistics staff officer. I was assigned as the logistics staff officer in charge on this horrific day. Our primary staff was thin and over tasked during this timeframe, mainly because we were heavily involved with the administrative, training and logistics preparations for our subordinate units that were headed for overseas deployments. In some cases, our subordinate units were coming and going from and to combat duties in the middle east.

This story is based on my recollection of various events that was filled with so much stress and chaos during the first 48 to 72 hours. The attack by the terrorists One World Trade Center (WTC 1) (the North Tower) was hit at 8:46 a.m. Eastern time and collapsed at 10:28 a.m. Two World Trade Center (WTC 2) (the South Tower) was hit at 9:03 a.m. and collapsed at 9:59 a.m. The resulting debris severely damaged or destroyed more than a dozen other adjacent and nearby structures. Every American was affected by this blow, the media showed video coverage of the 1st jet flown into the World Trade Center. Phone calls from family members were being received at our Headquarters 53rd Troop Command. The callers were asking if we knew anything about this. Phone calls were also concerned, if we knew the status of civilians that were employed at the World Trade Center. Never considering the idea that the first plane crash was an attack. First thoughts were, the commercial jet had malfunctioning problems. Meanwhile while thousands or maybe millions of Americans began putting on their TVs after the word got out about a commercial jetliner filled with passengers crashing into one of the largest New York City buildings filled with thousands of American workers. America suddenly was able to view live the second commercial jet liner blow right through the 2 World Trade Center at 9:03AM. Soldiers at my Headquarters were running up and down the corridors yelling, "We are being attacked" soldiers from all offices continued running up and down our halls sticking their heads in all the office rooms yelling, "we are being attacked." echoed through the corridors of our Headquarters. My emotions when the second plane hit WTC building #2 were a roller-coaster of a good dose of realism coupled with other emotions. For soldiers at our headquarters concerning this realistic attack, few of us never thought that this attack was going to end quickly. We all felt that our presence in the middle East somehow had to do with this attack. The Army National Guard was preparing for a full ground war, a ground attack following this air attack. Sadness of events followed quickly after the 1st plane hit. Almost as soon as the World Trade Center's Twin Towers fell on September 11, 2001, thousands of Army National Guard soldiers, firefighters, police officers, construction workers, and volunteers headed to Ground Zero to look for survivors. Every one of those first responders did the only humane thing they could think of. Because they didn't know how many people were trapped alive in the wreckage, soldiers and other rescue workers had to search carefully through the unstable piles of rubble for air pockets, called "voids," where they might find people who had been unable to escape from the collapsing buildings. To be safe, they didn't use any heavy equipment at first. Some dug with their bare hands, while others formed bucket brigades to move small amounts of debris as efficiently as possible. After the attack on the buildings, nothing was left but rubble. The site and weeks that followed were filled with smoke, flashing lights from emergency responders and the sounds of crews looking for bodies.

I asked for statements from various retired and some still active in the Army that were first responders on this day to give me their experience of that first day and all the days they were on duty to support the mission. so, you will hear from them as well. Before I take you to the chaos on September 11, 2001, I want to start from the beginning.

I want to take you back, way back to share with you, the inside. The places that the public don't get to see. It's a place where civilians that elect to choose the military as a career path begin. It's a place that changes personalities. I want to take you there and show you why our Army National Guard soldiers are more than ready, trained and able to rumble with anyone that tries to take away freedom from our country. These soldiers that I'm referring to are battle ready for any mission that involves protecting our country side and overseas wars. Our Army National Guard soldiers fight overseas to defend our homeland. One wonders how a civilian that you see in your everyday life can quickly put on a military uniform and become a soldier. The very same people that we see in the streets, those essential workers, firemen, police officers, plumbers, carpenters. One must wonder how can we send my electrician friend over to war, what does he or she know about fighting a war? Well, that is a great question. You see our soldiers are trained to deal with the difficult missions that are assigned to them. The strenuous and mental environment created by the United States Army and the Army National Guard jointly to prepare our soldiers for the rigors of combat and search and rescue missions during national disasters. I'll take you inside to show you how the United States Army school trains our Army National Guard soldiers, preparing them for the rigors of combat and national disasters. The type of training that focuses on unit cohesion, personal achievement, and mental and emotional resiliency. This only happens Inside, when soldiers are challenged to achieve a physical and mental best, bonds are built, happiness and misery are shared, and the organization is strengthened.

Find a comfortable seat when reading Command and Control. If your chair so happens to have seatbelts, well it's a good idea to buckle up for this ride that will land you straight to ground zero on September 11, 2001.

Chapter 1

Basic Combat Training-BCT (Inside)

Before I take you inside which is the Army's basic combat training-BCT, let me give you a general understanding of the Army National Guard. The following historical information, credits go to, "I am the Guard, a history of the Army National Guard, 1636-2000, forwarded by General John W. Vessey, Jr. "The Army National Guard in conjunction with the New York Air National Guard is an organized military force. It is also a federal military force of the United States Army. They are simultaneously part of two different organizations: The Army National Guard of New York state and each state in the USA, (also referred to as the *Militia of the United States*), and the Army National Guard of the United States (as part of the United States National Guard.) The Army National Guard is divided into subordinate units stationed in each U.S. state and territory, as well the District of Columbia, operating under their respective governors and governor-equivalents.

The foundation for what became the Army National Guard occurred in the city of Massachusetts, Salem in 1692, the first time

Command and Control

that a regiment of militia drilled for the common defense of a multi-community area.

The Army National Guard as currently authorized, organized and operates under Title 10 when under federal control, and Title 32 of the United State code and applicable state laws when under state control. The Army National Guard may be called up for active duty by the state or territorial governors to help respond to domestic emergencies and disasters, such as those caused by hurricanes, floods, and earthquakes, as well as civil disorder. The District of Columbia Army National Guard is a federal militia, controlled by the President of the United States with authority delegated to the Secretary of Defense, and through him to the Secretary of the Army.

Ron Sardanopoli

The President may also call up members and units of the Army National Guard, in its status as the militia of the several states, to repel invasion, suppress rebellion, or enforce federal laws. The Army National Guard of the United States is one of two organizations administered by the National Guard Unit the other being the Air National Guard of the United States. The Director of the Army National Guard is the head of the organization, and reports to the Chief of the National Guard Bureau. Because the Army National Guard is both the militia of the several states and a federal reserve component of the Army, neither the Chief of the National Guard Bureau nor the Director of the Army National Guard "commands" it. This operational command authority is performed in each state or territory,

Command and Control

and in the District of Columbia by the Commanding General of the District of Columbia National Guard when a unit is in its militia status.

While under federal activation, the operational command authority is transferred to the commanders of the unified combatant command who command all U.S. forces within their area of responsibility. The Chief of the Army National Guard Bureau and the Director of the Army National Guard serve as the channel of communications between the Department of the Army and the Army National Guard in each state and territory, and administers federal programs, policies, and resources for the National Guard."

Before you join the National Guard, you'll need to take a standardized test called, Armed Services

Ron Sardanopoli

Vocational Aptitude Battery-ASVAB.

Every applicant has to take the ASVAB, so it's not designed to intimidate you (it's not supposed to). It's designed to help the Army determine your strengths, to find where the individual applicant fit best and be most likely to succeed. The test measures your knowledge in eight areas: General Science, Arithmetic Reasoning, Word Knowledge, Comprehension, Mathematics, Electronics, Auto and Shop - Car maintenance and repair, and Mechanical. The results of this exam will determine where the Army can place the individual to begin their military career. The results will create your Army enlisted Military Occupational Specialties (MOS). Each MOS requires advance individual training and specialization. Army jobs can be divided into two basic categories: those that participate in combat missions and those that support the soldiers who are in combat roles.

When I took my ASVAB test a bunch of career fields were available for me. Only one involved participating in a combat mission, others were more related to supporting soldiers who have combat roles. Those other careers that I qualified for were more spread out in the administrations, and logistics careers. You will find out later what I selected for my career path.

Every Army National Guard soldier needs to be physically and mentally fit for combat training, and to be able to deal with the stress, and physical fitness required to jump into situations for national disasters. They will learn to follow the same rules and principles, team work and discipline and how to handle a weapon as the active Army soldier. They will experience stress and also test their limits. This all is extremely important as it pertains to the readiness for overseas conflicts to include combat missions in Afghanistan and Iraq. Also, for any response to emergency national disasters or civil disturbance.

Let's take a look from the beginning the challenges that I endured during combat training, along with every new recruit from the Army National Guard experienced.

The traditional National Guard soldiers are ordered to active duty as trainees. Once they are sworn in, they are given a rank of Private E-1. They are referred to as, trainees because they don't have the skills to be a soldier according to

Command and Control

the Army training program. They are transported

to an Army military installation for their Army

Basic training – BCT military post. Before the 1st

official day of training begins trainees report to

their reception station away from home

somewhere in the USA. At the reception station

the trainees are assigned sleeping quarters

where they get to chat and introduce themselves

to each of the trainees that arrived from various

states in the USA. The beginning of socializing

with many types of trainees and get introduced

to many new personalities, and cultures that

exists in the USA. You begin noticing all the

different accents from each the trainees, and we

all began detecting what state each soldier lived

just by their accents.

Ron Sardanopoli

We were trainees a perfect name given to a civilian's first day on active duty in the Army. At this point you feel like you have your big boy pants on and can't wait to write home to your friends, girlfriend or family to share with them how easy Army Basic training has been. Yes, I remember it quite clearly. Getting our 1-minute haircuts, barbers used noisy electric razors and after 5 or 6 swipes to your scalp down to the skin, we all had bald heads. That was the original Army haircuts. Getting fitted for our new uniforms both dress and combat uniforms. Everyone got their physical examination. We all got three square meals a day at the mess hall. But hold on, during my first meal I ran into a bit of a confrontation in the mess hall during the reception station assignment. When I went through the mess hall

Command and Control

line on my first day for my 1st meal at Fort Campbell Kentucky August 19, 1968, I drew a smile, just a friendly gesture to a regular Army private first class-PFC cook in the mess hall. This Army cook was a server, dishing out a portion of the lunch meal on the chow line. His response back to my friendly gesture was not a friendly one. He locks eye contact with me and said, "let me tell you something trainee, when you meet your drill sergeant, you're going to wipe that shit ass grin right off your face". I was shocked to hear this, and I was extremely embarrassed, my face was getting warm, I felt my face getting hot, my temper getting slightly out of control. At that very moment I stopped walking and held up the chow line. I stared back at that fella that made an un called for remark. I just stared him down, and didn't move. Thinking, "should I throw my tray over the glass partition separating the chow line from the food, then jump over the counter and begin beating the living crap out of him?" Soon after this cook made this wise comment, the entire regular Army of cook servers saw and heard the commotion. Every Army cook server alongside this wise guy private first-class heckler joined in and continued to laugh out loud. One voice yelling, "keep moving trainee you're holding up the chow line." Another server Army cook, called out to me and said, "Hey trainee you're not on vacation, welcome to the Army." With that comment the entire Army cook staff got another good hearty laugh out of his comment. Still standing and staring at the Army cook that made the first comment. I really was not paying attention to what the Army cooks were signaling to me. I was just totally pissed off and embarrassed on how his comment was delivered and it brought so much negative attention on me. I continued to stare right into that cooks' eyes, boy was I close to winding up in the stockade (Army jail). I continued to stare him down as I was holding my lunch tray, my head was ready to explode. Suddenly my new trainee friend from Arkansas was lined up on the chow line behind me began pushing me forward with his dinner tray. Arkansas said, in a loud whisper "stop staring at the cook, he has authority and outranks all of us, let it go." The trainee from Arkansas helped me cancel out the anger mindset that was building in me, and brought me more to my senses. I began to walk toward the dinner table, but my head was still turned around not in the direction I was walking, but in the direction of the Army cook that made the wise remark. That was my way to let him know that he pissed me off, and somehow, I wanted revenge. At eighteen years old I had so much piss and vinegar in me, well as we aged, we phrase it more like, "wanting to be treated the way you treat others". You could forget about that philosophy at Basic Training, as my story continues you will see treatment is never fair. At the end of the night at bed call, I called out to my friend from Arkansas, "Hey Arkansas," he answered, "Yeah New York," "thanks for watching out for me at the Mess hall, I almost lost it." Arkansas said, "I saw, no problem we need to stick together and reserve our strength for our first day of training."

The first day of basic training, who can ever forget the first day meeting our very demanding drill sergeants. We had our newly issued military clothing and equipment packed in our duffle bag preparing to leave the reception area. Buses showed up at 5:30am by our barracks to pick us up and transport us to our new basic training compound. There were no storage compartments at the bottom of the Army buses. So, we had to carry on these overstuffed duffle bags filled with newly issued Army clothing and equipment. It was a very hot Kentucky morning, we were all very anxious, and I'm sure there was some fear mixed into the anxiousness because of the unknown. During reception station many trainees shared their scary stories of what they heard about the first day of basic training. So, the night before our first day of training I was anxious thinking about what the next day will bring. The bus drivers showed up at our reception station compound to drive all the trainees to their perspective basic training compound. The bus driver was asked questions by some of the trainees during the ride. Hey bus driver, "tells us about what this first day is all about?" Everyone on the bus had their eyes on the bus driver hoping to hear for some kind of response to better prepare ourselves to what is about to happen. Questions from the trainees continue to be yelled out then there was total silence as the bus driver did not volunteer any response to the questions. The bus driver didn't answer any questions, nothing worth of any value to help us. He just smiled every once in a while. I was seated midway on the bus just past the second door and had an Aisle seat. I had a clear view of the bus driver through his rear-view mirror. Every once in a while, the bus driver would use his rear-view mirror to look at all the trainees, maybe he is just enjoying the moment, or is he actually making sure that everyone is seated in a safe position? All of a sudden, he put on the most suspicious smile. I don't know if it was a bit of paranoia creeping into me, but the suspicious smile was beginning to translate to, "believe me you have no idea, smiles." I knew we were somehow doomed. When we arrived at the barracks basic training compound, the bus driver shut off the bus engine. Everyone on the bus was quiet I kept my eyes on the bus driver as he knows more about our destination than anyone else. Then there was this loud familiar noise of the bus doors automatically opening both the front door and the rear door. Suddenly the bus driver quickly moved and ran down the stairs of the bus to exit. Yes, the bus driver vanished. He left a bus loaded with apprehensive and fearful trainees. Now we are all beginning to panic as we sit and wait. Sitting in a bus squished with overloaded duffle bags and the body heat to include the heat of a hot Kentucky summer day. Surrounded by six old world war I barracks, there was no trace of any human life. There were five other buses filled with trainees along with the bus I was riding in. It felt like we were being set up for what is yet to come. It was a perfect spot to be ambushed by enemy forces. It was so hot, beads of sweat continued to pour down my face and the faces of the trainees. The faces of the trainees looked anxious prompting themselves to the front of their bus seat and holding on to top backs of the seats in front of them, to establish a secure stable position in front of them to get a clear view of what was going on outside the bus. Not one of the trainees said a word, total quiet, all of our heads were turning to both sides of the bus looking out our windows for some kind of movement or sound, trying to figure out what was going on. Looking like we were getting ready for the world to end. A trainee now and then would shout out, "What now?", "getting scary", "I don't see anybody", "Let's get this over with dam it!" but otherwise total silence continues. All of a sudden, in a timed execution a bunch of drill sergeants all at the same time from all six barracks that surround our busses come charging down a short flight of stairs wearing their traditional head gear, uniformed smokey the bear hats, pouring out of all the compound barracks to surrounded the buses, they charged all of our buses yelling and screaming like a bunch of wild and angry soldiers. Some jumped from the outside and stuck their heads through the bus windows right into our faces. They were allowed to curse at us during this Vietnam war era training time and began ordering, well shouting out stuff like, "yawl &%#*&# flea bitten maggots" get off the bus, you're moving too slow, double-time." Picture everyone getting off their seats with our overstuffed duffle bags, squished pushing to get off the bus. A drill sergeant blocked the back door of the bus, and ordered everyone to file off the bus using the front door. Trainees falling to the floor of the bus, one trainee was walked on while being pushed to the floor. I was next to walk on him, but I waited and yelled out to him, "get up off the floor," he did. I had to brace myself by holding on to the bus bar seats to my left and right to hold back the trainees behind me that was pushing me off the bus. I was able to hold on long enough so the trainee that fell to the bus floor could get back on his feet. The trainees behind me were pissed off trying to push me out of the way with their duffle bags. The trainees were so scared and wanted to show the drill sergeants, how fast they were by following orders. The panic mode sets in, the mindset that every man was fending for themselves. Trainees just walking over other trainees that fell to the floor of the bus, because they were being pushed by the trainee behind them trying to get off the bus. Some of the drill sergeants' shouts that I remember were, "Get off this bus, you're moving too slow" and those that began filing off the bus were told, "You're walking? Double time(run), drop give me pushups." A few couldn't move fast enough climbing down the stairs of the bus with their oversized duffle bags and tripped and fell to the ground. A drill sergeant said, "You can't even climb down a short set of steps, stay on the ground and give me pushups". The drill sergeants gathered all the trainees between the buildings in formation and informed us the company we

Command and Control

belong to. The drill sergeants lined us all up in formation and said, "look around you, and we all turned our heads. These are the trainees you will be spending the rest of your time with." That's when I found out that I belonged to Company E, 4th Battalion. 1st Brigade. Then the yelling started up again, but this time it was with more intensity, as angry drill sergeants began asking a trainee in formation questions and when the trainee answered by saying, "yes sir or no sir" boy were they in trouble. Drill sergeants yelling, "Don't ever call me sir, I'm not an officer, I work for a living I'm a sergeant". I thought at the time, this is a strange way to teach us the difference in responding to an officer verses an enlisted man. An officer is referred to a sir, and an enlisted man based on their rank is called by their rank. So,

these drill sergeants wanted to be called
sergeant. We began the entire morning, dropping
for pushups, and if you answered a question
incorrectly and you had no more pushup strength
in you, you had to raise your duffle bag over your
head and double time around the compound.
The drill sergeants put together trick questions so
when you answered it incorrectly you had to
drop for pushups and demoralize you while you
were doing those pushups. They continued to yell
out various rules how things are done in the
Army. I witnessed some trainees fainting from
heat exhaustion, while they were running around
the barracks with their duffle bag over their
heads. The stress level was through the roof. if
you were overweight and because of your excess
weight you had a hard time doing pushups, those

trainees got the worst of the harassment. The drill sergeants were jumping on every minor infraction that the trainees conducted, if it didn't fall under the Army rules and regulations. To think that every 8 weeks another group of trainees follow this miserable training, and many have completed this horrible non stopping harassment before our training cycle. they have done this with every new trainee group that reports in on the 1st day. Those demanding drill sergeants continued to yell and scream orders the entire morning. I noticed that over 300 soldiers were being disciplined at the same time. Everyone was dropping for pushups and running around the compound like chickens without their head. Duffle bags raised over their heads just because of some kind of infraction designed by our drill sergeants. The drill sergeants told us, or should I use the expression, "warned us" not to ever be caught for the rest of our time of basic training walking through the compound, only double time, (running). There were only a few left remaining standing in formation. I was one of them, I tried to look straight, and listen to the reasons why trainees were getting reprimanded, thinking of any way that I could make myself invisible so to stay out of harm's way. Then it happened, as one drill sergeant looked at me, and swaggered his way towards me, he calls another drill sergeant over towards me. So now I have two of them walking in my direction. I'm standing at attention looking straight not an eyeball moving, breathing quietly, no facial expressions, and you could not stare at them, because that leads to, "who are you looking at?" I saw many trainees being reprimanded for moving their eyes to watch another drill sergeant reprimanding a trainee. I knew this was going to be a horrible experience. With the Kentucky hot sun to include the anxiety of being put through hell by these angry drill sergeants made me sweat perpetually. My heart was racing so loudly, I could hear the pounding of my heart beats when I held my breath to avoid any kind of movement. One drill sergeant approaches me and puts his face in front of my face as close as he could until the brim of his hat touched my far head. The drill sergeant said in a loud and aggressive manner, "tell me something trainee, everyone is dropping for pushups and running around the compound, but you are standing in formation like a prima donna. Do you think your someone special by standing here and not getting involved?" I yelled out, "no drill sergeant!" The other drill sergeant chimed in, it felt like the other drill sergeant was standing about the same distance of the one in front of me, by my left ear and yelled, "do you think your someone special? "I yelled out, "no drill sergeant!" their saliva was felt on my face with every thunderous word spoken. The drill sergeants brim of his smokey the bear hat was tapping my forehead as they were jolting their heads to be as loud and intimidating as possible. One drill sergeant said "did you just touch my head gear trainee? I said, "No drill sergeant" Are you lying to me trainee? "No drill sergeant" Now the two of them were yelling at me with degrading comments, "you think you're a soldier but you're not, you're at the bottom of the totem pole you're a grunt, you're a trainee, you have no authority." Both drill sergeants were now yelling in both my ears, yes, I had two of them screaming at me. One drill sergeant read my last name from my name tag its spelled, "Sardanopoli," but the drill sergeant pronounced it, "sergeant-Napoli." He yelled to a third drill sergeant, "Hey sergeant come over here and look at this trainee, he doesn't know anything about being a soldier and they made him a sergeant? "Meet sergeant-Napoli." Yes, now there is a third drill sergeant at this gathering. The third drill sergeant asked, "what state are you from trainee", my response was, "New York drill sergeant" "Do you live in the City of New York?' he asked, I said, "yes drill sergeant." It went downhill from there. One drill sergeant yelled out, "look what we got here a genuine New York city slicker that thinks he is a sergeant." I could not help it, I said to myself, "please lord do not make me laugh." My face began feeling hotter because I was holding my breath to try to hold in a laugh "Then it happened my lips started to quiver" All three drill sergeants theatrically motioned their body by raising their arms in the air, shaking their heads, as if they were in complete shock. Their body language to include their voices went into a louder uproar. Thinking, "here I am again the center attraction" I'm trying my best in staying out of harm's way and now I'm targeted for a direct hit by three angry drill sergeants. I felt like I was going to get hit with the most gut-wrenching harassment ever invented. One drill sergeant yelled out, "Is that a smile that you're trying to hold back trainee? You think I'm here to entertain you?" I yelled, "no drill sergeant" the other two drill sergeants answered his question simultaneously and said, "yes, this trainee thinks we are here to entertain him." All three yelled, "drop now trainee give me pushups and don't stop until I tell you to stop, count them out until I tell you to stop." I threw myself to the ground and I started counting my pushups, "one, two, three. A drill sergeant told me to stop, and he kneeled to the ground with his face behind my head and yelled, "one what? Two what?" I yelled out, "one drill sergeant, two drill sergeants." At one point I had all three drill sergeants surrounding my head continuing to yell all kinds of negative comments, demanding me to do physical and challenging pushups.

photo of what it looks like to be disciplined by three Army drill sergeants at the same time.

Command and Control

There were about 20 drill sergeants giving this type of discipline to all the trainees. It seems their plan was to make this first day one of our most miserable yet memorable experiences that you will never forget. It seemed to work for me as I am writing about it fifty-three years later. When my arms got tired from doing a bunch of pushups they began to tremble. I tried to do one more pushup but my chest slammed to the ground with no more strength to get back up, the drill sergeants never seemed to be satisfied, "your pathetic trainee" said one of the drill sergeants "lift your duffle bag over your head and run-in circles around the compound with the rest of your pathetic trainees." We were told to yell out some kind of chant that remind us that we are only trainees and we know nothing about being a soldier. But the drill sergeant's choice words to use in their chant is not appropriate for my story. More sit-ups, and running around the compound with our duffle bags over our heads. While I was running around the barracks with my duffle bag over my head, I was unlucky to have one drill sergeant escort me while running around the compound. This was all part of the drill sergeant's leadership and training techniques executed using the intimidation and harassment methods. This was an unforgettable first day.

Drill sergeants go to drill sergeant schools and are taught this kind of teaching strategy. It makes you feel that you have reached rock bottom, and they seem to be having fun doing it. Drill

is only one way to prove him wrong, is by showing him that we belong. By training hard, and stay motivated, and focused. SFC Vega promised us if you follow the Army basic training program you will experience a successful transition from a civilian to an army infantry soldier.

When the commander of the Basic Training compound arrived and addressed our Company E, he welcomed us. He gave us an overview about the training we would be receiving. He spoke in a way that brought back some of our dignity. It gave us a feeling that this horrible day is over, and now they will ease off on us. No such luck, once the commander left. SFC Vega had better things planned for us. He said that we have an abundance of duties that need to be conducted during our evening hours. In example, kitchen police – KP, the mess hall has a few dirty jobs that need to sparkle at the end of the duty day, cleaning the kitchen grease pit was the worst of them all. Peeling potatoes for the next day's meal. Also, because the barracks were old world war one-WW1 barracks and it is constructed of old dry wood. We had a fire watch duty to perform every evening. Walk around the compound with a flash light looking for fire hazards. We had a fire watch and compound security schedule resulting in reducing our sleep time to four to five hours a night. Formation every morning was at 4:30am, in the pitch dark of the morning for a long road march and fitness training before breakfast. With equipment packed on our backs, much of that road march involved periodic double timing that was when we all had to run in formation during the five-mile marches in our spanking new, not broken in yet combat boots, and at the same time sounding off various cadence started by our drill sergeants. Army cadence is a traditional call-and-response work song sung by the trainees while running or marching. Then the drill sergeants begin adlibbing those cadence songs to Jodie's. Jody is a recurring character that became a trainee traditional cadence. Jody refers to the man with whom a service man's wife or girlfriend cheats while he is deployed. Yes, those drill sergeants knew how to tear those trainees down to rock bottom. The cadence was a structured in a call and response in which one soldier initiate a song line, and the remaining soldiers complete it. It was also used as a work song when marching from one worksite to another worksite. The best affects I received from the call and response cadence was that its instilled teamwork and camaraderie amongst our unit members. On the fitness aspect of singing a cadence while running or marching helped me to keep my head up, take deeper breathes and exhale more forcefully. This seemed to increase oxygen to the lungs and gave the body more energy. This in turn makes the unit more healthy and better prepared. The road march ended back at the compound in front of the mess hall. After the unit was entirely exhausted, and more yelling by our demanding drill sergeants reminding us, "you all have failed, because each unit had stragglers that could not keep up with the others due to their physical inabilities. So, the entire Battalion had to drop for more pushups. Thinking, this must be part of the 3 weeks of continuous pushups that SFC Vega was talking about. The lesson learned here said by SFC Vega, "In the heat of combat never leave a brother soldier behind when they become exhausted or injured." From this point forward, each unit must volunteer a soldier to stay with the straggler until he catches up with the unit. Another new lesson on day 2. "Never leave a soldier behind." But wait it's not over, before every breakfast meal you had to swing a long rung of monkey bars before you can enter the mess hall to eat your meal. The drill sergeant dropped some more fear into these exhausted trainees by reminding us, "if you can't swing these rungs and you fall off between rungs, you don't get to eat your meal. Those that were not fit in the first week had to endure much more harassment by the drill sergeants, for those that could not swing those rungs, after trying over and over began developing blisters and eventually blood was wreaking through their blistered hands. Those that could not complete the rungs were subject to dropping for more pushups, and endure more harassment of being yelled at by those demanding drill sergeants, before they were allowed into the mess hall to eat their meal. Everyone eventually gets to eat their meal, thank god. The monkey bar challenge was cemented in place and designed to be used before every meal that was served at the compound. After the first week our entire company was able to climb those rungs before their meals. It was the Army's motivational way to develop the strength and skill to swing those rungs so you can eat your meal. It seemed to work, and they have been using that concept for many years. When we finally made it into the mess hall. Drill sergeants were making sure we grab only the food we eat. If there were leftovers in your plate, and tried to throw out the excess food. Drill sergeants will teach you only take what you can consume. I took too much butter on my first day and had to swallow a whole bunch of butter in an effort to learn to take what I can consume. Drill sergeants yelling at trainees on the chow line to keep shoulder to shoulder, no talking on the chow line, no talking at the dining table, take only what you can eat, eat and get out. With this Army invented diet plan, I lost 20 pounds during my eight-week training from 184 pounds to 164 pounds.

Basic training is designed to be highly intense and challenging. The challenge comes as much from the difficulty of physical training as it does from the psychological adjustment to an unfair way of life. Trainees are forged in the furnace of shared hardship and tough training. There were multiple road marches, a tough night infiltration course, a combat resupply event, a casualty evacuation drill, a pugil sticks competition, near the end of basic training, trainees spend a few hours facing off against each other in pugil stick bouts, its designed to attack your enemy after you run out of ammunition and are only left with your rifle and bayonet. For training the pugil sticks are padded training weapons. It's a battle with a selected opponent trainee on a platform in front of your unit members. Like a boxing match arena, company trainees rooting for their individual favorite to be knocked down by the other. ended when one knocks down the other and the other opponent could no longer continue. A four-day navigation course where trainees navigate about 46 miles, during this time they emphasize battle drills, tactical operations and numerous foot patrols. The idea is, total control, meaning the trainees every action is monitored and constantly corrected by drill sergeants. The drill sergeants also brief the trainees on Army customs and courtesies, drill and ceremony and the expectations of them while they are in training. The Army combat conditioning course is an excellent test of trainee's endurance, stamina, and physical fitness as they run across a variety of obstacles.

There is exercise that's built upon other skills such as squad tactics, medical training events, and Chemical, Biological & Nuclear (CBRN) confidence chamber. The trainees learned about their field protective mask or their gas mask.

Grenade training is taught, every aspect of the hand grenade, at the end of training each trainee throws two live hand grenades. The basics of rifle marksmanship, maintenance, and engaging targets at varying distances.

Rifle marksmanship is one of the most important instructions an infantry soldier will learn and never forget. Every soldier in the United States Army learns to become an infantry soldier. Our weapon is our only friend on the battle field.

Command and Control

There was a chant that SFC Vega our drill sergeant taught us and made us repeat it whenever he hears a soldier referring their rifle as a gun. Or if a soldier accidently has his rifle slip out of his hand and falls to the ground. Both situations happened to come to life on our very long training days at basic training. For instance, whenever you refer to your weapon by calling it a gun, look out. The heat will come directly to the trainee that mention gun instead of rifle. First and foremost, the closest drill sergeant stops all activity. He gets the attention to the entire company of troops. He gets into the face of the trainee that misused the word rifle and called it a gun. Immediately teaches the soldiers the difference between their rifle and their gun. He makes an example of the soldier sometimes by positioning him in front of the formation. The drill sergeant orders that individual to hold his rifle in the air with one hand and holding their crotch in the other hand, the chant goes something like this; "This is my rifle, this is my gun; this is for fighting and this is for fun." I know it made the individual look like a fool. If anyone cracked a smile and thought that was funny, which by the way, after duty hours in the barracks we thought that was hysterical. but if you were found laughing or grinning during training, you were doomed. They would drop you for more pushups until you can't do anymore, and definitely put you in the front of the Kitchen Police – KP detail list that very same day. Your weapon is the most serious piece of equipment that each soldier guards with their life. The Army taught us how to break down our entire rifle to every part that makes up the M14 rifle. Toward the later end of the Vietnam era around 1969, the Army modified the soldier's individual weapon, and its new model became the M16A1. Drill sergeants showed us how to break it down to the smallest part, clean it for inspection. We had to dismantle it to the smallest part, and assemble it.

Before I move on, I want to share a story about a trainee that I met at the reception station, the beginning of BCT. We met before we were issued our military clothing and received our haircuts. This trainee was from West Virginia, and introduced himself by saying his name followed by, "I'm a genuine hillbilly". So now his name was not his home state of West Virginia. He wanted to be called by his nickname, "Hillbilly." He was dressed like a poverty stricken, backward kind of appearance. Before his Army haircut, his hair was wild, and was trying to grow this grubby beard. He was wearing well-worn bib overalls and a straw cowboy hat. He flaunted this careless attitude with a lack of motivation. His image is still etched in my memory today. So, Hillbilly ended up being in the same basic training company E as I was assigned. He was one person I made sure I kept away from for many reasons. Because Hillbilly was so careless and had a hard time complying with the rules. The drill sergeant would make the entire company suffer the consequences of one soldier's mistakes. It's a way that we learn to build team and stick together. Also, if we have a problem with a soldier in our unit that is causing the unit to lose their free time privileges, drill sergeants want the trainees to take care of our own in-house problems. So, one evening while Hillbilly was on extra KP duty. The company designated (trainee) platoon sergeant formed a meeting with company trainees minus Hillbilly. He wanted to know how we were going to handle the problems Hillbilly is causing our unit. Our entire unit agreed that Hillbilly is making our unit fall behind in many of the Battalion competitions against each of the companies in the Battalion. Many crazy ideas were mention because so many of us are pissed off about his careless actions during the duty day. We wound up reminding each other of all the times he caused our units penalties, and punishment. Hillbilly and his wild antics that constantly slows down our training cycle and many of our privileges taken away. We even had a West Virginian trainee who was an outstanding trainee that tried to talk sense into Hillbilly. Those attempts came up with empty results. So, the majority of trainees in our barracks agreed that Hillbilly was going to receive a blanket party. For those civilians reading about blanket parties and are not sure what a blanket party is, let me explain. Back before and during the Vietnam war era time frame blanket parties was a successful way to motivate disgruntle trainees during their basic training cycle.

A blanket party was a form of (mob) discipline at the time that usually takes place in

a military barracks setting, typically in an open bay of a barracks. Blanket parties are no longer allowed in the military, blanket parties and other forms of corporal punishment are now illegal in the United States military and punishable under the Uniform Code of Military Justice. Let me explain how the blanket party was enforced. While the party recipient is sleeping, four trainees get an Army blanket and position the blanket over the recipient body from the neck to his feet. Two on one side of the bunk and two on the other side of the bunk, holding his body down on his bunk by holding and tightening the ends of the blanket. A fifth trainee positions himself in the front of the bunk to hold down the recipient's head with a towel over his mouth so nobody that's outside the barracks could hear him screaming. The entire barracks of trainees form two lines holding a heavy object (shoe, boot, etc.)

wrapped in a bath towel to use to strike the party recipient's body. The outcome is the recipients entire body becomes black and blue and he is in excruciating pain for a few days. We were planning to conduct the blanket party the next day after our scheduled weapons qualification. That evening when Hillbilly arrived to our barracks everyone was treating him a little differently, people just feeling disgusted about hearing his same tales. Hillbilly would tell a whole lot of crazy stories during the evening hours in the barracks. his growing up in the mountains of West Virginia. In his stories I overheard him saying he used outhouses as a rest room, he also walked around with a double barrel shotgun. He reminded me of someone out of the Hee Haw show, hosted by country music superstars Buck

Command and Control

Owens and Roy Clark. Both those guys embraced hillbilly antics and rural comedy for nearly 20 years. So, Hillbilly at times can put a smile on your face just because he acts crazy and just is not grasping the seriousness of how important this training is for all of us including himself. But it has gotten to a point that everyone realizes he is not pulling his load, and he don't care. Hillbilly could not wait taking his Army issued M14 rifle to the firing range to show his buddies a thing or two about firing a rifle. Many thought that Hillbilly was a time bomb ready to explode, especially when you give him live rounds for his rifle. As the company marched to the firing range the next morning to begin firing for our weapons qualification, guess who is on the firing line very close to me. Yes, Hillbilly was positioned one shooter away from me. The shooter that was positioned between Hillbilly and I signaled me that he was not happy about being positioned alongside Hillbilly. By this time of the basic training the drill sergeants already knew that Hillbilly is a problem, maybe a mental problem, well some referred to him as a headcase, and an accident waiting to happen. Hillbilly claims his paw (father) already taught him everything he knows about guns. By this time every trainee never referred to our weapon as a gun. Yes, Hillbilly never stopped calling a rifle a gun. Just to show you how difficult he was to comply with the Army program. After we completed all our firing tasks to complete our qualifications training and weapons qualification, everyone on the firing line was still. We were all told to remain in the prone position (chest to the ground and back up). I heard hillbilly gabbing away, the safety officer yelling out to Hillbilly, "silence on the range" The firing line had extra ammo that needed to be expended. The range officer allowed us to discharge the remaining rounds. So, everyone on the firing line hears the order to lock and load their last magazine of extra rounds. Before the next order by the range office was being ready to be announced, I could hear Hillbilly acting up getting excited, I could hear him feeling anxious about the idea to discharge the remaining ammo. The M14 rifle that we were issued had a selector switch that switches the rifle from semi-automatic to fully automatic. When the range officer together with the safety officer gave the command, "commence firing," to discharge the remaining ammo. Hillbilly jumped to his feet and pointed his weapon downrange towards the target. He was in a standing position that did not comply with any firing standing position we were taught while shooting of his M14 rifle. Hillbilly yelled out, "John Wayne" as if to let everyone know that he was emulating the actor John Wayne from one of his war movies. When he squeezed his trigger in the automatic weapon mode, his rifle was positioned at his waist level facing his weapon down range. Hillbilly could not handle the kick from all those rounds being fired. The bullets were being discharged automatically like a machine gun. He lost his balance, and fell on his backside, during his fall he accidently fired a round right through his foot and boot. I could not believe it; I took a quick look and saw that the bullet went right through his boot and foot, a small hole was in the ground so the bullet was not enlarged in his foot. The blood was rushing out of his boot. Hillbilly was in great pain, safety officers rushed to the scene, yelling out, "medic, medic," The range officer must have called for a medivac helicopter from the post hospital. The chopper arrived in ten minutes. They took his boot off, and it looked terrible, a gruesome sight. Hillbilly became another statistic of dropouts just like SFC Vega warned us. It solved the disgruntled trainee problem as the blanket party was postponed for that evening.

In Company E formation that evening, SFC Vega reminded us that we all witnessed another careless act by a careless trainee. Reminding us about sick, lame, lazy, and crazy drop outs. As far as Hillbilly is concerned, I suspect he could fall under the 4F category. You might have heard of a number letter combination used for categories as a reason for dishonorable discharge.

Classification 4F, the designation of 4F is a classification category under the Selective Service Classification System and it means that the individual has been rejected for military service as unfit for physical, mental, or moral reasons. Trainees never know why our trainee comrades' bunks are empty the next day. But for Hillbilly, we all knew why he was no longer with us.

Command and Control

Company E 4th Battalion 1st Brigade, graduation date October 11, 1968

This photo above is my graduation day from Basic

Training. It's easy to spot out the short senior drill

sergeant SFC Vega [front row second from the left]. He stands as you see in this photo with the same look. As serious as a heart attack. It was SFC Vega with his staff of demanding drill sergeants that made soldiers out of Company E 4th Battalion 1st Brigade. Every Army National Guard soldier had to endure the same training, and they all had their SFC Vega's to push them beyond limits that they thought was never possible. SFC Vega trained us so one day we too can be called sergeant, trainer of soldiers, backbone of the Army. SFC Vega trained us all in Company E to accept those responsibilities that are ours. He trained his soldiers to be the best defenders of freedom in the world. Most of all he trained me to be self-sufficient, that one day I may lead the

years old, big guns were more interesting than sitting behind a desk shuffling paperwork.

After successfully completing basic training at Fort Campbell, Kentucky, I received my orders to report to Fort Sill, Oklahoma. Each and every Army National Guard soldier began his military occupational service – MOS training – after the successful completion of basic training. I remember my airplane flight leaving Fort Campbell, heading to Fort Sill, Oklahoma. It was a commercial flight with the flight attendants offering passengers a mini glass bottle of liquor with a plastic cup of ice. Taste-size brand name spirits for free! These were tiny whiskey bottles that I've seen today priced at $5-$8. I was thinking, "I'm 18 now, just graduated from Army basic training, officially a soldier, old enough to fight in a war, and old enough to swig this mini whiskey down the hatch. Salut!" When the plane landed, an Army bus was waiting to pick us up and head to Fort Sill. The battalion sign entering Fort Sill said, "Welcome to the Field Artillery battalion, Fort Sill, Oklahoma – home of the Field Artillery." Our battalion motto was "Teamwork." It was here that I learned to be a leader and to be a member of a noble profession – a field artilleryman.

The mission of the battalion was to train soldiers in field artillery core competencies to provide proficient integrators of lethal and non-lethal fires to the operational force. One training battalion consisted of three distinct batteries which are what units are called in artillery. Those batteries house and train the military

Command and Control

occupational skills for the field artillery branch. Today those seven occupational skills have been changed because of today's modern technology. These new occupations are, Cannon Crewmember MOS 13B (soldier loads and fires howitzer), Field Artillery Automated Tactical Systems Specialist MOS 13D (soldiers operates advance field artillery tactical data systems), Fire Support Specialist MOS 13F (Fire support specialists help the Army determine where and how to deploy artillery in combat situations), Multiple Launch Rocket System Operations/Fire Direction MOS 13P (The MLRS launches various missiles and ammunition in quick strikes during combat, Field Artillery Fire finder Radar Operator MOS 13R (these soldiers detect enemy forces and alert Army units)Field Artillery

Ron Sardanopoli

Surveyor/Meteorological Crewmember MOS 13T (this soldier monitors weather conditions), Field Artillery Senior Sergeant MOS 13Z (Leads in fire support, operations/ intelligence, and target acquisition activities).

I looked forward to joining my new team. Arriving in Fort Sill after completing basic combat training school, I was highly motivated. Transitioning from a trainee to a soldier made me feel ready to take on any challenge the Army threw my way. Transitioning from civilian to soldier in the United States Army gave us all an important new mission to accomplish.

Briefed by our commander at Fort Sill, we were told that our unit has a high operational tempo - OPTEMPO." Things moved fast, we had to hit the ground running. Each day of training, we had to arrive at the unit ready to contribute. All my personnel actions had to be up-to-date. MEDPRO was my current readiness status. It is an Army medical protection system giving the status of every soldier's medical and dental data, making sure all were in good physical condition. Physical fitness was important; our team had to complete an Army Physical Fitness Test [APFT] for the record. The test was given to us within seven days of our arrival. We had all just completed Army basic training, so this fitness test was an easy one for most of us to pass. Leaving basic training made us feel like "lean, mean fighting machines."

One of the teachings in "teamwork battalion" was that we lead from the front. That means we demonstrate our leadership by going first. In some situations, the leader does the tuff things first to show it can be done. Showing is sometimes easier than telling. We had not had a day off since we were civilians, more than two months before. At formation at the command, parade rest, soldiers were told to relax with their two hands locked together behind their waist. This is the position soldiers are usually in to hear announcements that are important. The commander announced, "Saturday is a day off," and I heard the joyful whispering voices that were around me in formation. The soldiers reacted with jubilance, freedom and partying. We were being treated like soldiers and we were respected by our leaders. Now we are called privates, not trainees. What a great feeling of

recommended military occupational specialties [MOS], according to my ASFAB test results.

I interviewed for this position and got the job. I made a change from being a traditional part-time soldier with a civilian job in the financial district on Wall Street in Manhattan. I landed a government position. I became a government employee working fulltime for the Army National Guard, and by doing so, I changed my MOS from an artillery gunner to a position in the administrative supply field.

Eventually I began learning by experience and getting my military education by attending many quartermaster [supplies] schools at Fort Lee, Virginia. My promotions on the enlisted soldier rank began escalating eventually becoming the battalion supply sergeant, that promoted me to the enlisted rank of sergeant first class – E7, for the 105th Field Artillery Battalion. When I was assigned as a battalion supply sergeant, I knew I was holding onto a job in the logistics career field that was critical for our soldiers' readiness posture.

I took this responsibility with pride and honor and was promoted soon after. I was enjoying the challenges this career field threw my way, and eventually the battalion commander put me in for a vacant quartermaster warrant officer position. Nov. 1, 1976 I was promoted to warrant officer – WO1. My new position specialty at the time was the battalion property book officer. I became the accountant for all the property and

Command and Control

equipment owned by all the artillery unit [Battery] commanders.

Through the years serving as a quartermaster warrant officer with many years of logistics positions, I entered the Army's premiere logistics system of experts. My responsibilities took me to positions of leadership, training, mentoring and advising my commanding officers. I became a more confident leader and more mission oriented, and I became a subject matter expert. My years of development had included the highest military school required to reach the rank of chief warrant officer five – CW5 at Fort Rucker, Alabama. By earning my master's degree at the State University of New Paltz, New York, I surpassed the Army's requirement for civilian education. I reached the experience and educational levels that helped me support a multitude of Army missions.

Some soldiers call the warrant officer rank the best rank in the Army and that may be in dispute among soldiers of different ranks. Some have said the chief warrant officer – the CWO – is in a unique position between the officer corps personnel and the enlisted personnel. They're kind of neutral between the military ranks. Generally, warrant officers are pretty much left alone to do their jobs because of their technical expertise. Warrant Officers are higher in rank than enlisted personnel but lower than commissioned officers that rank 2nd Lieutenant and above. Warrant officers make up the technical foundation of a U.S. military service branch. Throughout their careers, they specialize

Command and Control

in a technical area such as special operations, intelligence, aviation, food service, transportation or military police. Although they make up a very small group in military service, warrant officers have a large responsibility that includes training soldiers, organizing and advising on missions, and advancing with their career specialties.

I know of a few former/retired enlisted men and officers who said if they could have done it over, they would have become a warrant officer. They also said they'd recommend others who are technical experts in a field and qualified, to go that career route. I think the most popular and sought-after career fields in the warrant officer corps are flight warrant officer/pilot, CID special agent or Army intelligence.

Ron Sardanopoli

Fast forward to 1985 when the United States Army instituted a new generation of software and computers to support property accountability for non-expendable equipment and repair parts. To do this, the Army went to a major re-organization to form a Material Management Center – MMC – under every Army division headquarters in the United States. The Army took from each division all the logistics experts – mostly logistics warrant officers and enlisted personnel – and formed an MMC.

This new generation of computers had a mainframe computer that was housed in a semi-trailer and was designed to function in a combat environment at the Army division level. This new Army active-duty position was designed to manage a logistics automation center to support the entire 42D Infantry Division. I was selected to supervise this mainframe computer for the 42D Infantry Division Material Management Center – MMC.

This was an active-duty position title 10 [title 10, a funding code given to active army personnel]. This mainframe computer serviced 125 units and close to 37,500 troops. This computer got the division soldiers their combat equipment, Meals Ready to Eat [MRE], helicopter parts, flashlight batteries – you name it, this mainframe computer did the work. Getting all these things in their varieties and shapes and sizes, and getting them out to the soldiers who needed them, was a big job.

Ron Sardanopoli

While assigned to this position, I was promoted to chief warrant officer four – CW4 – the highest grade of the warrant officer ranks at that time.

1995: The old generation of mainframe computers was gone and the new generation gave each unit and soldier their own laptop computers to take care of their own supply needs.

The 42-D Infantry Division Material Management Center – MMC – disbanded and all the logistic soldiers who supported this logistics command were transferred to the 53rd Troop Command Headquarters and the 42D Infantry Division Headquarters. All working for the general staff's [G-4] logistics office. I became one of those soldiers that was transferred to Headquarters 53rd Troop Command.

Meanwhile, Dec. 1, 1991, the Army created the chief warrant officer 5 [CW5], the [new] highest warrant officer rank in the Army. The position was created to have a master level technical and tactical expert who can perform the duties of a technical leader which meant manager, integrator and advisor. I was honored to be selected for this new position, logistics manager 53rd Troop Command, and new rank of Chief Warrant Officer five – CW5. I became a primary staff member for the Commander of the 53rd Troop Command. CW5s are the senior technical experts in their branches and serve at brigade and higher levels. Usually, the CW5 position is filled by a lieutenant colonel so this promotion came with an abundance of responsibilities. I was selected by Col. James D. McIntosh who was a full bird Colonel, and the Chief of Staff of the 53rd Troop Command at the time. Col. McIntosh's vision for the military alignment when it came to training, administrations and logistics was noteworthy. Believing in the U.S. Army's newest warrant officer corps rank, CW5, was monumental to the Warrant Officer Corp.

Once Col McIntosh arrived as our new chief of staff, he immediately laid out his expectations for how logistics should be conducted in a major Army command. Col. McIntosh's day-to-day operations as chief of staff was commendable. He was an all-star chief of staff. His institutional knowledge of the Army National Guard coupled with his extremely high competency level of leadership, training, administrations and logistics made him a strong asset to our headquarters and the New York Army National Guard. Because of his noteworthy contributions to the Army National Guard, Col McIntosh was brevetted to Brigadier General [1 star] at his retirement ceremony.

BG [R] McIntosh once told me, "I believe in you and together we can improve the logistics posture of the 53rd Troop Command Headquarters." I also give accolades to our commanding general at the time, Brig. Gen. John L. Jones for his keen selection of our newest Chief of Staff Col. James D. McIntosh. BG Jones, a highly intelligent leader, and his number one concern was to care for his soldiers. He'd often visit his primary staff officers at his Headquarters just to deliver a positive, uplifting message to start our duty day. We all knew that Gen. Jones and our Chief of Staff Col. McIntosh were meeting to discuss important issues and concerns related to our missions. It was this commander together with our chief of staff who believed in the Warrant Officer Corps and adapted a chief warrant officer-5 CW5 to the 53rd Troop Command primary staff.

On the morning of Wednesday, Aug. 13, 1997, my most trusted senior non-commissioned officer [NCO] MSG Dominick Ciccarielli came to my office with "that face" he put on so well. He was pretty much a quiet leader to staff and through the years serving alongside him, I learned to read his facial expressions. The expression I saw this day was not a good one. It was the one he has just before he dishes out bad news. Yes, that face – the one he gives which means if we don't react to the situation now, it'll only get worse.

MSG Ciccarielli had a tremendous logistics vision and could see something go wrong before it actually happened. I always checked with him before I reacted to a problem in the field. That morning, I was on a very important call with a subordinate unit commander. The commander reported that he completed his property inventory and that he and his soldiers were ready for their overseas deployment mission. Walking to my desk, Master Sergeant - MSG Ciccarielli heard me ending my phone call with the unit commander and there was that look again. "What now, MSG?" I asked, knowing something was possibly wrong. He took a deep breath and said, "Chief, the commander of the 53rd Troop Command, General Jones, wants to see you in his office as soon as possible." I asked him, "why," thinking, "we never want bad news to get to our commander before we can fix the problem." I said, "MSG, you've been my interceptor and we always intercept and fix our logistics before things go wrong, and before it reaches our commander. Jumping out of my seat, I asked, "is there a soldier who filed an Inspector General- IG complaint?" IG complaints are Inspector general complaints. They are critical complaints that go straight to the commanding general's desk, and higher. MSG Ciccarielli said, "I have no idea why the commander wanted to see you, sir."

Usually, it would have been the Chief of Staff Col. McIntosh who would want to see me about important critical issues. I wondered why BG Jones would contact my senior master sergeant to call me into his office. I checked again with my primary staff members but they knew nothing about anything being wrong in our logistics pipeline. I even went to our Chief of Staff Col. McIntosh's office to ask the Chief if he knew anything about why General Jones wanted to see me. Col. McIntosh's secretary said, "Chief Sardanopoli, the Colonel stepped out of his office and I don't know where he is?"

Ron Sardanopoli

Walking to the commander's office, I noticed MSG Ciccarelli following a few paces behind me, still holding onto his cold-as-stone facial expression. Thinking and feeling anxious, my brain was reviewing all the ongoing troop maneuvers, doing a memory scan to make sure I crossed the Ts and dotted the I's. When I knocked on the door, Gen. Jones' deep commanding voice told me to come in. When I opened the door, it took a few seconds for me to realize what the meeting was about.

Chief of Staff Col. McIntosh immediately brought the group in the room to the order of attention. A personnel officer read my promotion order to chief warrant five – CW5 – out loud. It was my official private promotion pinning ceremony to chief warrant five.

Command and Control

The picture that captured this moment is of Brig.
Gen. John. L. Jones [right] and Chief of Staff of
the 53rd Troop Command Co. James D. McIntosh
[Left] CW5 Ron Sardanopoli [center]. And oh yes,
my senior NCO MSG Ciccarielli who carried the
camera to take the picture.

Ron Sardanopoli

Pinning ceremony BG (R) John L. Jones (Right), CW5 (R) Ron Sardanopoli (Center) BG (R) James D. McIntosh (Left)

Command and Control

I told my Master Sergeant, "You got me, Master Sergeant," and we both got a good laugh. I received my promotion orders and my new military position, logistics manager 53rd Troop Command.

In my new position, I had the privilege to work alongside Major [P] Edelman, the P standing for "promotable." Who was Major Edelman? On Feb. 1, 1996, he filled a vacancy left in the lieutenant colonel position and became the commanding general's primary staff officer in charge of manpower [G-1].

Maj. [P] Edelman led the administrative side of the 53rd Troop Command. He worked his way up the enlisted ranks as a personnel staff NCO [E-7] In 1978, he was commissioned as a 2nd lieutenant after graduating from the Fort Benning Officers Candidate School. He approached his daily workload challenges with lots of creative resolutions. He was considered an officer at the top of his game when it came to manpower and personnel administration. Our commander, BG John L. Jones, Col James D. McIntosh, and staff, welcomed him with opened arms.

Maj. Edelman was promoted to lieutenant colonel-LTC in March 1977, assigned as deputy chief of staff for the 53rd Troop Command. As we move forward in this story, you'll see how LTC Edelman became a main ingredient who helped our primary staff of officers and enlisted become a strong primary staff for the 53rd Troop Command.

Chapter 4

Guard deployments increase

In 1999, the Army National Guard and Army Reserve units became a major force for overseas deployment because the active Army military manpower began shrinking. The frequency of military operations had greatly increased. For example, the U.S. Army in Europe had shrunk by nearly 70% - from 213,000 Army personnel in 1990 to about 62,000 in 1999. Yet, military deployments dramatically increased.

The USAREUR -United States Army Europe and Africa, a component of the Army is responsible for directing United States Army operations throughout the U.S. European command and the U.S. African command. It has participated in only 29 peace-keeping or humanitarian missions. However, from 1991, which marked the end of the Gulf War, to 1999, USAREUR participated in more than 100 such missions.

For the headquarters 53rd Troop Command and its subordinate units, In addition to supporting these primarily peace-keeping and humanitarian military operations, our subordinate units still had to maintain their combat readiness which usually involved field training exercises.

Thus, upon returning from an overseas military deployment, many solders begin preparing for field training immediately, along with the remaining 53rd Troop Command units. Always maintaining the unit's combat-ready posture, preparedness is the number one priority.

Every subordinate unit must earn its METL – a mission essential task list. The METL is a list of tasks that a unit must accomplish in combat. It is a written requirement of wartime missions. Again, the purpose of this training is to prepare our units for combat. The Army National Guard has proven active duty for disaster relief, or humanitarian purposes, and coupled with overseas deployments, really tested their abilities and responses to natural or man-made disasters and homeland defense missions.

Our headquarters, the 53rd Troop Command, was and still is a command-and-control headquarters. At the end of 1999, the Headquarters 53rd Troop Command were in command and control of 51 subordinate units [see flow chart].

Command and Control

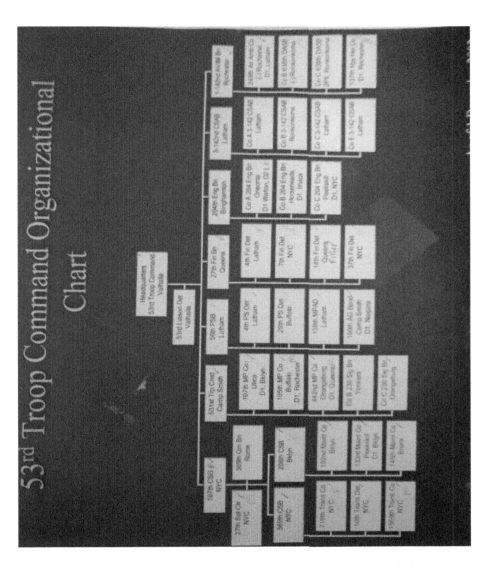

A total of 51 subordinate units under the command and control of

Headquarters 53rd Troop Command

Ron Sardanopoli

Our newly-appointed commander, Brigadier General Edward G. Klein became the Commander of the 53rd Troop Command. BG Klein prior military assignments derived from the 101 Cavalry Regiment. According to Wikipedia, "The 101st Cavalry Regiment is a unit of the New York Army National Guard, and has existed in various forms since 1838 which saw service in the American civil war, the Mexican border conflict, World War I, World War II, and Afghanistan." When I first came face to face with BG Klein in a briefing room to review the current logistics status of the 53rd Troop Command. I couldn't help but noticing his issued Army combat boots were designed differently than everyone else's combat boots. He was wearing the tankers boots.

Command and Control

Why are they called tanker boots? According to Wikipedia, "The reason why tanker boots were manufactured for tanker soldiers was to allow circulation to crew-members feet, as they may be sitting or immobile for long periods of time. Tank crewmen during the Gulf War reported remaining seated at their gunners, drivers, and commanders' stations for up to the entire 14 hour of ground combat." BG Klein coming from a cavalry combat unit, gave our chief of staff and primary staff an awareness that a leader from a historical combat organization was chosen to lead the 53rd Troop Command. A leader with his credentials was needed during a time that overseas conflicts are heating up in the middle east, and around the world. With the escalation of conflicts in the Middle East and around the world so became the escalation of our work load at our Headquarters.

BG Klein's primary staff officers at the time, for manpower the [G-1] was Jaquelyn Russell. LTC Russell was an asset to the general's primary staff. She had institutional knowledge coupled with her administrative knowledge and immediately became an asset to the general's primary staff.

In training, [G-3] was a young and upcoming creative thinker, LTC William Bodt. He was an officer who thought outside the box and developed many new ideas to assist our subordinate units to reach their training goals. This led to many successful deployments.

Command and Control

In logistics, [G-4], there was Major Simon Hu, a traditional part-time soldier who had just recently been selected for this position. I was handling the day-to-day logistics activity for the G-4, keeping Maj. Hu abreast of my daily activities by phone, email and the weekly and monthly drills he was required to attend. Maj. Hu's civilian career was a programmer analyst for Morgan Stanley, a top financial institution. In 1997, the merger of Morgan Stanley Group, Inc. and Dean Witter, Discover & Co. created the world's largest securities firm in the world. On a sidenote, Maj. Hu's office, while working for Morgan Stanley, was located in Building #5 of the World Trade Center, and you will read more about Maj. Hu later in this book.

Ron Sardanopoli

Each of the three 53rd Troop Command's fulltime primary staff members, LTC Russell, LTC Bodt and I, fell under the leadership of our Acting Chief of Staff – AcoS LTC [P] Robert E. Edelman. A colonel, Thomas Sweeney, was a traditional soldier who filled the chief of staff position. Col. Sweeney civilian job was Deputy Commissioner of Homeland Security with the NYPD. As in the past, all traditional soldiers relied on the fulltime (day to day) representative to keep them abreast of all operations. LTC [P] Edelman kept. Col. Sweeney up-to-date in the day-to-day activities. Eventually, LTC [P] Robert M. Edelman was promoted to colonel and was assigned as Chief of Staff, 53rd Troop Command and was one of the Command's most dynamic chiefs of staffs. COL Edelman understood how the Army National

Command and Control

Guard institution operated. Working Monday through Sunday, he enforced all the Army's policies, plans and projections. He molded the general's primary staff into one that was prepared for all kinds of readiness missions. His decision making was always for the improvement of the organization, and his decisions was always the right ones. But what made Col. Edelman stand out was that he made our senior headquarters officers and senior enlisted feel like he was steering the ship with confidence and continued to position our headquarters to complete successful missions. Under his watch as Chief of Staff of the 53rd Troop Command, he maintained a very high success rate in completing our missions. He had the trust from our state headquarters, the 53rd Troop Commands subordinate commands, his primary staff, as well as all the commanders he worked under, for and with. It was his knowledge of how the Army National Guard functions that helped to guide our ship. In a recent communication exchange with Brigadier General - BG Klein and I, he said, "During 9/11, when Col. Robert Edelman was the troop commander chief of staff, he was my primary advisor. Col. Edelman's institutional knowledge was invaluable to all of us at the 53rd Troop Command."

In this book, you'll learn more about our Commander BG Klein's excellent leadership and quick decision- making during times of duress. When we had BG Klein and Col. Edelman as commander and chief of staff, the 53rd Troop Command, state headquarters seemed to call on our units for state missions more often than the other state Army headquarters.

Headquarters 53rd Troop Command kept its subordinate units at a very high readiness posture. Much of the credit for those standards goes to the officers and enlisted personnel who worked in the training, personnel and logistics primary staff sections.

Every three months, Col. Edelman had his primary staff inspect the current unit status and readiness of our subordinate units. Each primary staff member, i.e., LTC Bodt, training; LTC Russell, manpower; and me, logistics, would inspect subordinate commands readiness status to help them maintain a higher level of readiness.

In logistics, we exercised the Command Supply Discipline Program – CSDP. This program was designed to provide the necessary tools for subordinate unit commanders to successfully address the relationship of good logistical processes and operations achievements which are reached by stressing good supply discipline. Our primary staff worked together during our visits to the subordinate commands, always finding ways to interact face-to-face with the subordinate units and command to improve their readiness posture.

Each quarter, the logistics staff invited every supply sergeant in the fifty-one subordinate units to our day-long logistics conference located at our headquarters facility. We reviewed the basic supply procedures. Our goal was to show them how to get their supplies as quickly as possible. My logistics staff and I were always finding various ways to keep 51 subordinate units in a high state of logistics readiness for deployment.

LTC Russell spent countless days and nights working the headcounts needed for the units to reach their readiness goals. LTC Russell had two efficient staff members, SFC Raul Lopez and SSG Patricia Farrington, who were by her side to assist on delivering her plans and policies.

LTC Bodt made sure all soldiers were qualified to operate effectively and affectively on the job before deployment. He managed unit training schedules to make sure that our headquarters and our subordinate units soldiers got the training needed for deployment, and that training included weapons qualifications. LTC Bodt provided the necessary training for our soldiers to be qualified in their military occupation skill - MOS. He also had two efficient staff members, SGM Carl Fitje and MSG Tom Lambert to assist on delivering his plans and policies.

I managed the logistics side to make sure our units had the necessary clothing and equipment at 100% fill so the unit could perform their missions. I would be remiss if I didn't mention four critical staff members who were extremely excellent soldiers from our logistics enlisted corps. MSG Dominick Ciccarelli had an enormous amount of knowledge and experience in the logistics field and when he retired, his replacement, MSG Frank Kania, who was also a very knowledgeable and experienced logistics enlisted soldier. CW4 Anthony Baldi was our centralized property book officer who provided visibility of all military equipment for all 51 subordinate units. CW4 Gerard Wieczorek [deceased] provided bus transportation for all soldiers going to and from deployments or training sites. Chief Wieczorek also collected food service data from all our subordinate units. SFC Douglas Marcantonio was our supply sergeant and special project NCO.

When units received their orders from headquarters in Washington through our state headquarters to deploy overseas, our primary staff spent endless days and nights working to help those units reach their goals. We brought primary key soldiers who represented those deploying units into our gatherings to be face-to-face with our staff. Those meetings started six months before the units deployed and included reviewing their readiness status and making laundry lists of areas that need improvement in their manpower, equipment, general supplies, and MOS-trained soldiers.

Our staff's priority was to fill shortages as soon as possible to get our units ready to deploy. Constantly measuring how they were progressing on their state of deployment readiness, we did this from the first day they received their deployment orders from Washington until the day of their deployment, always keeping an open communications link with the deploying key personnel.

Command and Control

Our units, including maintenance companies, transportation companies and military police companies, were needed by the active Army components. The Army was falling short of logistic units. At times, the Army requested some of our military police units to assist them overseas.

Our engineer units were also called upon, but our most active units going overseas for multiple tours were our transportation units. These transportation units fell under the command and control of the 369th Corps Support Group. The 369th Infantry regiment, formerly known as the 15th New York Army National Guard Regiment, is a historical military organization, commonly referred to as the Harlem Hellfighters. According to The Harlem Hellfighters on www.history.com,

Ron Sardanopoli

"They were an infantry regiment of the New York National Guard during World War I and World War II. The Hellfighters spent more time in combat than any other American unit. Comprised mostly of African-American soldiers, the 369th Infantry regiment spent 191 days in the frontline trenches and suffered 1,500 casualties, the most losses of any American regiment. The soldiers of the regiment were given their nickname, Harlem Hellfighters, by the German enemies because of the regiment's ferocity and tenacity in battle. However, it took the Army more than 100 years to recognize the unit's official designation as the Harlem Hellfighters. On Sept. 11, 2020, the Army Center of Military History recognized the 369th Infantry and its descendent, the 369th Sustainment Brigade, as the Harlem Hellfighters.

Command and Control

The 369th nickname is now observed as a historical, traditional name. The special designation program that made the Hellfighters an official name is now operated by the Unit History branch of the Army Center of Military

Ron Sardanopoli

History.

The United States Army certifying that, "Harlem Hellfighters" become the traditional designation for Headquarters and Headquarters Company, 369th Sustainment Brigade

Chapter 5

National Disasters

The thought of a national disaster happening in the State of New York was a faraway concept. To task our soldiers with more soldering in emergency situations was an unwelcome thought. So much time had passed since 1993 when the World Trade Center complex, consisting of seven buildings with 293 floors of office space, housed some 1,200 companies and organizations. Each floor of the Twin Towers had more than an acre of office space. The complex included 239 elevators and 71 escalators. The World Trade Center housed about 50,000 office workers and averaged 90,000 visitors every day. The below-ground mall was the largest enclosed shopping mall in Lower Manhattan, and was the main interior pedestrian circulation level for the World Trade Center complex. About 150,000 people a day used the three subway stations below the towers in the mall.

The below-ground parking garage included space for 2,000 vehicles but only 1,000 were used on a daily basis. The number of parking spaces was reduced for safety and security reasons. This was after terrorists drove a truck packed with 1,100 pounds of explosives into the basement parking garage in 1993, setting off a blast that killed six and injured 1,000 people.

The New York Army National Guard was not ordered to a full mobilization for that attack. Meanwhile, the need to mobilize more of our units for overseas deployments continued to escalate. They were needed for more overseas missions; some were preparing to deploy and some were returning from deployment. Washington began to increase its use of the Army National Guard to fill in for regular Army deployments.

We began seeing orders asking for a second deployment for the same units that returned two years before. It was getting crazy and extremely stressful for the individual traditional Army

Ron Sardanopoli

National Guard soldier who had a fulltime civilian
job.

That soldier was asked to leave his family for a
second deployment that was an average of six to
eight months. Eventually, civilian companies had
a hard time holding positions for those deployed
soldiers.

We had ongoing activation of small cells of
National Guard soldiers on state active-
duty support missions for various
communities. Many of those missions were
because of ice storms, tornados, forest fires, etc.,
going on in the cold north country of New York.
Our soldiers were on duty in New York State for
state missions, and were also sent overseas for
federal missions. The thought of adding a major

national disaster emergency call-up to our soldiers' workloads was an unwelcome thought. There was a national disaster scare about 21 years ago when we were all worried that we'd soon be living in the Stone Age again. We thought all our computers would be hacked and shut down as soon as the clock struck one second past midnight on New Year's Eve, Dec. 31, 1999.

It was referred to as the Y2K bug and at the time, it was a real scare. The scenario that caused the panic was that the world as we knew it would essentially come to an end in the wee hours of the morning of Jan. 1, 2000.

It was believed that the complex computer programs first written in the 1960s were written with a two-digit code, leaving out the "19." As the year 2000 drew near, people feared that the computers wouldn't interpret "00" of the year correctly. This would cause a major glitch in the computer systems all over the world.

Many people thought the systems would be able to operate past Dec. 31, 1999, and the two 0s of the year 2000 would incorrectly be interpreted as Jan. 1, 1900.

The entire New York Army National Guard was on alert because this would cause power plants to stop operating properly, banks to incorrectly calculate interest and airline schedules to be blanked out, not to mention serious concerns with security of nuclear power plants and more. Some countries spent millions of dollars setting up bunkers in case of catastrophic breakdowns. We put all our subordinate commands on alert. On Dec. 31, 1999, the entire

Command and Control

headquarters' primary staff and its subordinate staff set up a Tactical Operation Center – TOC – in the heart of New York City at the Park Avenue Armory, waiting for the clock to strike midnight, the beginning of the year 2000.

We were all ready to respond to any national disaster that Y2K wanted to deliver. We were the shakers and movers of the 53rd. We were present and accounted for, including our Commander BG Klein, Chief of Staff COL Edelman, G-1 LTC Russell, SFC Raul Lopez, G-3 LTC Bodt, SGM Carl Fitje, G-4 Maj. Hu and I, along with MSG Ciccarielli. There were others, both enlisted and officers, who deserve honorable mention as team staff members and important military personnel.

We all stationed ourselves in a New York City armory, a historical landmark from the days of the 7th Regiment. We were designated as in "Command and Control" of this Y2K potential national disaster.

Our Commander Brigadier General Klein coordinated with two important 53rd Troop command officers who had very high civilian positions with the NYPD and the NYFD.

BG Klein began to establish relationships with key New York police and fire-fighting officers and established an excellent bond for coordination of any future New York City national disasters.

The 107th Support Group Armory, [Park Ave NYC] is where we set up the TOC. Tactical operations center usually includes a small group of specially-trained military personnel who guide members of a tactical element during a mission.

Command and Control

Our TOC included a command post that had officers in the communications field. Army-issued radios powered by 10KW trailered generators were set up. Our TOC officers were positioned in such a way as to enable line-of-site communication between team members.

Our primary staff had open communication with state headquarters and our subordinate units in the areas of G-1 manpower, G-3 movement and maneuver and G-4, logistics.

Generator power and antennas strategically placed were set up to communicate with all our subordinate units. Those units were in various locations in the State of New York in the event that power and communication were lost.

The communication was tested. It worked. It was getting closer to midnight. The Time Square ball was ready to drop, bringing in the new year, 2000. Missing were the revelry and the shoulder-to-shoulder crowds that typify Times Square on New Year's Eve. That was replaced with empty streets and an eerie quiet as the final minutes of 1999 ticked away. When the clock struck midnight on Jan. 1, 2000, we all held our breaths as if an explosion was about to happen. We looked at each other to see if anyone heard something that sounded like an explosion. We looked to see if our lights were flickering, an indication of power loss. We heard or saw nothing to indicate the year 2000 would cause problems for computer systems around the world.

I peeked through the armory facility window and saw only two teenagers who seemed oblivious to any Y2K concerns. They were shooting off Roman candles and firecrackers and celebrating the new year, 2000.

Meantime, the staff members at the TOC realized our global computers did not fail us. There was no computer crisis. There were no more concerns that communication and transportation would break down. There was tremendous relief written on every face.

Lessons learned from this Y2K false alarm became epic. Y2K helped us realize we could be better prepared for a national disaster emergency.

We learned that units needed a huge administrative work project to update their national disaster soldiers' contact list. Because of our traditional soldiers' changes of address, reassignments, transfers, etc., our subordinate

units could have had a difficult time performing a

quick response to a total emergency

mobilization, if needed.

The Y2K alert had our units contact all their

soldiers and eventually were able to get their

personal locator information, and alert lists up to

date.

Subordinate units made sure their personal

locator information for their unit was up-to-date

and accurate. Y2K had each soldier

briefed about the necessary steps to keep their

families safe and physically/financially secure,

should they be called to duty.

Family members were reminded they could get

help from the Red Cross if necessary.

Command and Control

Headquarters 53rd Troop Command became a task force for New York City during this Y2K alert. The 53rd Troop Command task force assigned our headquarters in Command and Control of New York City Army National Guard units, we picked up more units that fell under the 42nd Infantry Division command because they were located in the New York City area.

By BG Klein setting up territorial task forces with state headquarters, the 53rd Troop Command gained 42nd Infantry Division Battalions, the 1st Battalion, 101st Cavalry from Staten Island, New York, the 1st Battalion 258th Field Artillery from Queens, New York, and the 1st Battalion, 69th Infantry, New York, NY [Manhattan].

The 69th Infantry was located just two miles north of what would soon become Ground Zero. The remaining units under the 53rd Troop Command task force were subordinate units of the 53rd Troop Command.

Our Commander BG Klein established the ground work in New York City as a result of his and state headquarters planning for Y2K. It was decided they would form a regional task force because New York is unique in that it has the Army Guard, the New York Naval Militia – which is Marine and Navy, - and also, New York has the state defense force which is the New York Army National Guard.

Because of Y2K, state headquarters set up regional task forces with Long Island as Task Force 1, the New York City area being Task Force 2 and Stuart Air Force Base being Task Force 3. They also established task force locations for the remaining territories west and north of New York City.

BG Klein continued to lay future ground work for any future national disasters. He established relationships with the NYPD and the NYFD. And, he continued to improve our readiness in case of any potential future disaster.

BG Klein was working on getting our soldiers to react to a national disaster with a quicker response. Three months prior to Sept. 11, 2001, BG Klein met with the head of New York City's director of emergency management office, Chief Richard Sheirer.

Chief Sheirer began his long career as a fire alarm dispatcher in the New York City fire department, working his way up to deputy commissioner in 1994.

Ron Sardanopoli

In 2000, Mayor Rudolph Giuliani named Chief Richard Sheirer Director of the Mayor's Office of Emergency Management. There were conversations to establish better communication between the New York Army National Guard, the New York City Police Department and the New York City Fire Department.

Chief Sheirer was in agreement with BG Klein's recommendations.

BG Klein didn't stop there. Two or three weeks prior to 9/11, a decision was made to put an Army National Guard desk in the mayor's Office of Emergency Management. New York City now has an office in the mayor's Office of Emergency Management in case of any future national disasters. The location was Building 7 World Trade Center, New York City.

Command and Control

Meanwhile, at our home station, our commander, coordinating with his Chief of Staff Col. Edelman, tasked our G-3 LTC Bodt to establish a war room. This room would out-perform any Tactical Operation Center. It would be open to the commander and his primary staff for clear communication. The room would also be able to handle work stations for our entire primary and their subordinate staff members. The room needed furniture, state-of-the-art computers, automatic briefing devises, flat screen TV's lights, phones, FAXs, etc. It also needed a briefing platform to host briefers who could be seen and heard by any attendee, no matter where they are located in the war room.

Ron Sardanopoli

When this room was completed, it would be used for our emergency operating center – EOC – in case of any future national disasters.

LTC William Bodt got the order and delivered big time!

This EOC was a very large, open, rectangle room. It was eerie and cold looking when you went in alone. The walls were large cement blocks. The double entrance and exit doors were constructed with heavy steel.

The room was built like a weapons or ammunition storage room. Because of the room's sensitivity, and because we worked with both classified and unclassified documents, our physical security officer made sure the room used the necessary security locks leading into the EOC.

Command and Control

This room provided office space for at least 70 or 80 primary staff officers and enlisted personnel. LTC Bodt turned this room into a state-of-the-art war room with up-to-date automation, just as the commander ordered. It was very well done, but everyone was hoping there wouldn't be any catastrophic events, that would require the need use this room.

Every so often, LTC Bodt would call in a representative from the State Emergency Management Office [SEMO] to work with our primary staff as a training event, role playing a catastrophic event.

Being that as the crow flies, we were about four miles from the Con Edison nuclear power plant in Peekskill, New York, we role played that a flawed reactor design at the plant caused a nuclear accident. We used the results and statistics from the Chernobyl disaster in the Ukraine as a training aid. We also used this room as training for a state mission and live but small state active-duty missions from time to time. But if a national disaster causing total mobilization was eminent, we were ready.

Chapter 6

Terrorist Attack

On Sept. 11, 2001, 19 militants associated with the Islamic extremist group Al Qaeda highjacked four airplanes and carried out suicide attacks against targets in the United States. Two of the planes were flown into the Twin Towers of the World Trade Center in New York City. A third plane hit the Pentagon just outside Washington,

Command and Control

D.C. and the fourth plane crashed in a field in

Shanksville, Pennsylvania.

Almost 3,000 people were killed during the 9/11

terrorist attacks which triggered major

U.S. initiatives to combat terrorism, and defined

the presidency of George W. Bush.

This is the timeline of the 9/11 attacks:

8:15 a.m. Flight 11 was commandeered;

8:42 a.m. Flight 175 was commandeered;

8:46 a.m. Flight 77 was commandeered;

8:46 a.m. 1 World Trade Center was hit by a 747

jetliner;

9:03 a.m. 2 World Trade Center was hit by a 747

jetliner;

9:16 a.m. Flight 93 was commandeered;

9:38 a.m. The Pentagon was hit by a jetliner;

9:59 a.m. 2 World Trade Center was leveled;

Ron Sardanopoli

10:28 a.m. 1 World Trade Center was leveled.

World Trade Center [WTC]

On Sept. 11, 2001, in New York City at 8:46 a.m. on a clear Tuesday morning, an American Airlines Boeing 767 loaded with 20,000 gallons of jet fuel crashed into the north tower of the World Trade Center in New York City.

The impact left a gaping, burning hole near the 80th floor of the 110-story skyscraper, instantly killing hundreds of people and trapping hundreds more on the higher floors.

The State General of the New York Army National Guard contacted Brigadier General Klein to alert him that the first plane crash would more than likely cause the Army National Guard to mobilize. The adjutant general told BG Klein to head down to the World Trade Center and find out more about the status.

BG Klein jumped into a HUMMV – a military tactical vehicle – and bolted down to the WTC. By the time he arrived, getting through the chaos and traffic, the second plane had already hit WTC Building 2 and New York Gov. George Pataki had already ordered 2,400 soldiers to state active duty.

I was on duty at the 53rd Troop Command, "command and control headquarters," at the time. As the evacuation of the tower and its twin got underway, television cameras broadcasted live images of what initially appeared to be a freak accident. Then, 18 minutes after the first plane hit, a second Boeing 767 – United Airlines Flight 175 – appeared out of the sky, turned sharply towards the World Trade Center and sliced into the south tower near the 60th floor. The collision caused a massive explosion that showered burning debris over surrounding buildings and onto the streets below.

It was clear that America was under attack. Firefighters from the NYFD rushed to the WTC minutes after the first plane struck the north tower. By 9 a.m., shortly before United Airlines Flight 175 hit the south tower, the NYFD Chief arrived and took command.

The initial response of the NYFD was a rescue and evacuation of the Twin Towers occupants which involved sending firefighters up to assist people who were trapped, including in elevators.

Command and Control

Problems with radio communications caused fire commanders to lose contact. The repeater system in the WTC, required for portable radio signals to transmit reliably, was malfunctioning after the impact of the planes. And, many off-duty firefighters arrived to help, without their radios.

When the south tower collapsed at 9:59 a.m., firefighters in the north tower were not aware of what had happened. The battalion chief in the north tower lobby immediately issued an order over the radio for firefighters in the tower to evacuate, but many did not hear the order, due to the faulty radios. As a result, 343 firefighters died in the collapse of the towers.

Ron Sardanopoli

On a rescue and evacuation mission, NYFD rushed to the WTC minutes after the first plane struck the north tower. By 9 a.m., shortly before United Airlines Flight 175 hit the south tower, the NYFD Chief arrived and took command.

Command and Control

Camen Taylor, AP

18 minutes after the first plane hit, a second Boeing 767 – United Airlines Flight 175 – appeared out of the sky, turned sharply towards the WTC and sliced into the south tower near the 60th floor.

As the disaster unfolded, New York State's Commander in Chief, Gov. George E.

Pataki, ordered thousands of New York Army National Guard troops in the New York City and surrounding upstate onto state active duty to provide direct support to local authorities in a search and rescue mission.

As Y2K lessons learned and future planning took effect, the New York's 53rd Troop Command Headquarters was given the helm to be in command and control of all the New York City Army National Guard units placed on active duty, including National Guard soldiers added from surrounding upstate units.

Because of the mindset of Army National Guard soldiers, they responded to the search and rescue mission immediately after the second plane hit. Many did not even wait for formal orders to mobilize, with many going to their home station armories and hundreds going straight to Ground Zero with their uniform and gear.

Mayor Giuliani ordered "all New York City civilians to leave the island of Manhattan."

Photo of Twin Tower survivors leaving Manhattan

Ron Sardanopoli

I was able to catch up with some of the Army National Guard first responders to share their memories of this horrific attack.

This is a narrative from Master Sergeant Joe Grado [Ret.], a first responder from the New York National Guard, reflecting back to that horrific day:

"Well, it started out as another day working as a temporary shop foreman of a military maintenance shop – OMS-9 – in Jamaica, Queens.

I was just getting the jobs for the day collected when I heard one of my men say that a plane had hit the WTC. We had the TV on in the break room. I figured it was a small plane like a Cessna, but it turned out to be a larger plane. All hell broke loose, especially when the other tower was hit. All the full-time workers started getting things together, getting the HUMMVs fueled and running, opening the arms room, calling to mobilize soldiers by the Alpha Roster, because they knew help was needed at Ground Zero. In the meantime, I called my wife to pack me a bag that I'd pick up soon. My armory was in Williamsburg, Brooklyn, the 206 Corps Support Battalion. The only authorized people on the parkway were police, fire and military personnel. I had to show my ID card to get on and I went about 80 mph after I did. At that speed, I reached the armory pretty quick. While crossing the Bklyn Battery Tunnel which was right across the river, I couldn't believe what I was looking at. The smoke, the fire, the gray clouds from all the debris coming down - Oh my God, this is for real. When I reached the Marcy Ave. Armory, everybody was going in different directions. I proceeded to our orderly room and reported in. At that time, we had to set up our Tactical Operations Center -TOC – and had a meeting with the commander about what to do. We then contacted our subordinate maintenance companies, and the 145th Maintenance Company, for a situation report [SitRep] and personnel and equipment accountability.

I took a HUMMV along with some of my soldiers and we went to Ground Zero. Upon arriving, we saw all the people running away from the Ground Zero location. As we got closer, everything as far as the eye could see was covered in gray ash, all one color. When we looked down the street, we saw twisted metal beams. We then went back

to the Marcy Ave. Armory to get things rolling.

Setting up the TOC at the armory went well. We

started to gather information from supported

units and waited for instructions from the

commander.

"The next day, we had all the commanders arrive

at the Marcy Ave. Armory for a meeting and

instructions were assigned to each unit.

After a few days, our tasks were to make sure the

perimeter around Ground Zero was secured. Our

soldiers manned one of the makeshift piers to

assist families who had loved ones affected

and hadn't heard from them. We tried to give

them a status report and this was very hard on

everyone. My job was to assist the operations

officer handing out missions as they came in and

to check daily on Ground Zero soldiers. After three weeks, we closed up shop and went back to civilian life."

Many small cells of National Guard soldiers who had armories in the heart of Manhattan close to Ground Zero created small teams to join and supplement the NYPD and the NYFD. The chain of command communications was extremely weak, as the collapse of the WTC building had a mobile antenna installed on its roof.

So, soldiers and other rescue workers at Ground Zero were brainstorming on the very first day as to what their next actions should be.

The most senior military commanding officer on site was given the authority by BG Klein to make those decisions. As feedback trickled in to the

Command and Control

53rd Troop Command about the status of our soldiers at Ground Zero, it was described as "total chaos, soldiers were afraid to breath in the air." Soldiers used their Army-issued gas masks to prevent any possible inhaling of unwanted chemicals in the air. The smell was described as "a burning smell but something more, difficult to describe."

In the first days and nights, Guard men and women worked with bucket brigades, joining many rescue workers removing debris by hand while searching for survivors. They reported finding civilian men's shoes and high-heeled women's shoes, shoes that belonged to those who perished on that day. A total of 2,996 people died in these attacks, including the 19 terrorists.

Ron Sardanopoli

New York Army National Guard soldiers join the rescue workers by forming
bucket brigades at Ground Zero.

Command and Control

Now that the 53rd Troop Command Emergency Operating Center [EOC] was in full operation at our headquarters, all military cells in New York City would be reporting into our headquarters based in Valhalla, New York.

The 53rd Troop Command EOC was 30 miles north of Ground Zero. Brigadier General Klein had already received a phone call from the New York Army National Guard Adjutant General after the first plane hit. BG Klein made his way to Ground Zero, knowing that in a disaster of that caliber, the New York Army National Guard was going to be called in.

Additional supporting command and support units included the 369th Harlem Hellfighters and the 206th Corps Support Battalions, the 145th Maintenance Company and the

642nd Aviation Support Battalion. The 105th,

107th and 442nd military police companies

deployed as well.

BG Klein needed heavier equipment to help move

heavy pieces of the buildings, and more soldiers

were mobilized to operate the equipment.

Within hours, the number of troops at logistical

and support sites, armories and air bases, swelled

from hundreds to thousands. At its peak, more

than 3,500 Guard troops were serving in the New

York area alone.

Even as the World Trade Centers crashed to the

ground and dazed survivors were being carried

through the rubble, members of New York's

Army and Air National Guard were already on the

scene, working with civilian emergency

responders.

Command and Control

New York City area troops, including those who were also NYC police officers and firefighters who are soldiers with the New York Army National Guard, were already on their civilian jobs working under incredible conditions, trying to save lives. Members of the "Fighting 69th Infantry" rushed to their Lexington Avenue Armory which is only blocks from Ground Zero. Forty-eight hours later, the Lexington Avenue Armory was designated as a reception center for families of the missing. From there, soldiers went directly to the scene. An immediate call to the 53rd Troop Command reported that at least five New York Army National Guard troops and two Air National Guard members were listed among the missing or killed at Ground Zero.

Ron Sardanopoli

The hundreds of troops from the 69th Infantry were soon joined by other troops from the various boroughs. Tankers from the Staten Island-based 1st Battalion, 101st Cavalry and cannoneers from the 1st Battalion, 258th Field Artillery from Queens and the Bronx, along with troops from the Queens-based Company C, 1st Battalion, 105th Infantry were among the Guard's joint task force.

Troops were geographically hours away from Ground Zero, reinforced and supported by troops from the Binghamton-based 204th Engineer Battalion, the Buffalo-based 152nd Engineer Battalion and Air Guard men and women from the civil engineer squadrons from the state's five Air Guard bases.

Command and Control

Eventually, soldiers with their individual commanders were forming small cells to create affective support elements in the search and rescue mission.

At the helm was New York's 53rd Troop Command Headquarters, based in the Westchester County community of Valhalla, 30 miles north of the city. Forward command and control came from the Guard's 107th Corps Support group at the park Avenue Armory. This unit is the direct descendant of the famed Seventh Regiment – the unit that gave the Guard its name. After a few days, additional equipment to move heavy debris was needed. We had to activate additional upstate units that had the equipment and expertise to help with the mission.

Ron Sardanopoli

The headcount for duty swelled to more than 4,000 soldiers.

It was amazing the way everyone came together to get the job of providing security and saving lives to Lower Manhattan done.

Whether it was a mixture of Guard troops, NYPD, firefighters, construction workers or volunteers, everyone had just one thing in mind and that was to save lives.

Soldiers used the debris from the fallen buildings at Ground Zero to rest their heads every chance they could, pacing themselves so they can continue into the wee hours of the night.

Command and Control

Soldiers used the debris from the fallen buildings at Ground Zero to rest their heads.

Chapter 7

Perimeter Defense

BG Klein's task force's geographical concept was in effect for the Army National Guard. Units in the same geographical New York City areas from different Army commands worked together to protect their communities and save lives. BG Klein's relationships established with the police, coupled with his already-established excellence in military leadership, was making progress. Making his NYPD already-established contacts helped getting organized at a very fast pace. He maneuvered soldiers in various hot spots to address emergency situations, putting out many fires. He established a security perimeter around Ground Zero with the NYPD.

The evening of Sept. 11 and the entire day of Sept. 12, troops worked on the rubble pile with the NYFD, the NYPD and many civilian emergency responders. The first responders referred to that mission as the bucket brigade, trying to locate survivors. After the first 48 hours, some troops shifted to perimeter security.

Command and Control

World Trade Center Building 7, the original New York Emergency Management Center, was destroyed in the attack. Eventually, Pier 92 became New York City's emergency operation center with more than 150 agencies and organizations either operating in or connected to the emergency center. BG Klein assigned LTC Andrew Leiter [Ret.] and LTC John Flanagan [Ret.] as the liaisons representing the New York Army National Guard. They both worked the Army National Guard desk so the NYPD and NYFD could quickly relay any missions to our Army National Guard's liaisons officer. I was able to make contact with Col. Leiter who provided this narrative:

"I was one of the first National Guard officers activated on Sept. 11, just after the second plane hit the WTC. My normal M-Day position – [an M-Day member is an Army National Guard or Air National Guard member who performs weekend military drills, but is not on fulltime duty] was as a liaison officer to NYC [1998-2003]. I was sent to NYPD headquarters on 9/11 and worked there until Saturday, Sept. 15. I was moved to Pier 92, the replacement for the NYC Emergency Management Office which was lost when the World Trade Center Building 7 was destroyed. I was stationed there through Nov. 2 when my active-duty tour ended."

One of the 53rd Troop Command's subordinate battalions, the 2nd Battalion 1/53rd Troop Command was called to duty. They have qualified military police units and soldiers. Many of these soldiers are traditional soldiers with civilian jobs as police officers.

All three of those military police units were activated and ordered to Ground Zero to help with the policing needed. Here is a testimony from Master Sergeant Don Tucciariello. MSG [Ret.] Tucciariello worked for the S-3 operations office, responsible for operations of subordinate units belonging to 2nd Battalion 53rd Troop Command. MSG [R] Tucciariello making sure all of his subordinate units contacted their soldiers to let them know that a full mobilization was in effect. MSG Tucciariello headed straight down to Ground Zero to see if he could help give his soldiers more information about their mission. I was able to chat with him about his experience of being mobilized to Ground Zero. Here is his narrative as he reflects back almost 20 years ago:

"Well, to the best of my recollection, I was in my office at Camp Smith, Peekskill, New York. I was the operations sergeant for the 2nd Battalion 1/53rd Troop Command which had, under its command, the following units: 104th MP Co., Utica, New York; 105th MP Co., Buffalo, New York; 442nd MP Co., Orangeburg, New York, and the 101st Signal Bn, Orangeburg, New York. At about 8:55 a.m. that fatal morning, I received a phone call from one of my subordinate units telling me to turn on my TV. It was a horrible site to see. Not sure what was going on, I saw on live TV the second plane strike the second tower.
"My thoughts were one of shock at first, then I remember thinking life as we knew it was over.

Command and Control

Land lines for telephones were not operating, but somehow, cell phones were still up and running. After consulting with the few people from our staff and the command structure, a decision was made to activate the three MP units. We communicated via cell phones to the representatives of each unit to activate and bring their soldiers into the armories. After many hours of coordinating, I felt the need to do more. So, since the wheels were in motion to bring our soldiers in, I put my MP brassard on, jumped into one of our military vehicles and headed for the World Trade Center site.

The scene, upon arriving, was beyond belief. There was debris and twisted steel everywhere. Firemen were digging frantically through the piles of debris looking to save the lives of those who were thought to surely be trapped. There were dozens of ambulances waiting to take the injured to area hospitals. As I walked around the area surveying the devastation, I ran into another soldier who I knew from the fighting 69th. That unit was actually the closest to the site. Their armory was on Lexington Avenue and 14th Street in NYC. We greeted each other with an embrace. It was good to see a familiar face amongst such devastation. Continuing my walk, I noticed civilians taking pictures of the area, and that didn't seem right to me on several levels. Were they recording the devastation for a terrorist organization or to sell to the press or TV news agencies? I, along with a National Guard chaplain in the area, asked those people to leave the area. After several hours and into the darkness, I returned to my headquarters in Peekskill to get some rest. In the meantime, throughout the day, MP units had continued to mobilize and organize.

Our first MP company was driving down the New York State Thruway where I met them at the NYC border just south of the Yonkers Raceway. The NYC police escorted us down the thruway to the Henry Hudson Parkway. It was a clear, sunny day and while driving along the Hudson River, you could see the plume of ash making its way across the sky westerly towards the Statue of Liberty. A sad site to see. As we approached south of about 14th Street, there were people lining both sides of the roadway applauding our arrival. They seemed to be looking for any signs of hope, and the Army National Guard's arrival seemed to give them just that. Upon our arrival, a perimeter was set up to keep onlookers and anyone who was not a first responder out of the area. We set up a TOC [tactical operations center] outside a NYC public school on West Street. An entrance to the immediate area known as The Pit was established and entry was strictly enforced. Anyone who was not a first responder who wanted access to this sensitive area was referred to the New York City EOC, the Emergency Operations Center. At the time, that EOC was located in the 57th Street and West Side Highway area. Meetings were held for National Guard leadership in several locations. One that stands out was the armory of the 69th Infantry on Levington Avenue and 14th Street. I parked on Lexington and it wasn't easy to walk past the photographs of missing loved ones. The pictures had been hung there by family members pleading for knowledge of their whereabouts. Relatives were there begging for any information or assistance anyone could provide to find their family member. It was heartbreaking and a memory soon not forgotten.

One day on my rounds checking on soldiers in the area of the pit, I was talking with an FBI agent and a NYFD chief when there were three blasts of a truck horn. Panic set in as this was a signal of a blast and everyone ran for cover. I wound up in a doorway and saw a soldier running my way. I grabbed him into the safety of the doorway also. It turned out that the horn was a false alarm, but people were so on edge. It turned out the soldier was a reservist from the Fort Monmouth Army post area who put on his uniform and wanted to help. There were several military volunteers just like him in the area. In the days to follow, all three MP companies were on location, initially traveling back and forth to Camp Smith in Peekskill to sleep. The Jacob Javits Center on 34th Street and the West Side Highway became available for the National Guard to sleep and eat there. The military police troops performed a number of missions. At the beginning, on the evening of 9/11 and the entire day of Sept. 12, troops worked on the rubble pile with civilian emergency responders trying to locate survivors. After the first 48 hours, the troops shifted to perimeter security, local traffic control and logistics, life support and administrative support tasks at the request of city officials. These missions continued throughout the entire clean-up."

Command and Control

The 53rd Troop Command commander BG Klein had cells of soldiers helping out with the bucket brigade trying to find survivors, but at the same time he was establishing force protection. There were a couple thousand soldiers who were used to helping the NYPD. According to the NYPD, the first thing they needed from the New York Army National Guard was to form a perimeter around the crime scene. The reason: The crime scene had to be sealed. The police operated in radio cars, not units. The NYPD was unable to seal the crime scene. The chief of police said to BG Klein, "This is what we would like from you, can you seal off the perimeter?"

It took 2,000 Army National Guard soldiers to seal off the crime scene. Initially, BG Klein ordered the first arrivals of four battalions on line. A vast section of New York City was sealed off. Work at the bucket brigades was slowed by hellish bursts of flame and the collapse of the last standing section of one of the towers taken out by the twin suicide commercial airline jets. Then, in coordination with the NYPD, they realized the perimeter was too big. They began shrinking it down and each day the perimeter would shrink down.

On the first day of the attack, all the electricity in the ground zero area was knocked out. The attack caused all communications and New York City based cell phones with the New York City area codes to be knocked out. None of the street lights in the surrounding area were working. Our soldiers were getting anxious about this defense perimeter idea because the governor's orders did not call for weapons and ammo to be used by the Army National Guard. In the meantime, local commanders had a plan in case the air attack was going to be followed by a ground attack. The New York Army National Guard had weapons and ammo very close to them in disclosed locations. Local commanders provided feedback to BG Klein liaisons working with the NYPD.

The concern was that in parts of the perimeter, there were soldiers with no weapons, and no police officers were visible in case of a land attack by terrorist groups.

BG Klein immediately reacted to this concern and called John Ardomat, the deputy commissioner for the City of New York. BG Klein met with the deputy commission to walk the perimeter, and he did it for two reasons. One, for the morale of the soldiers, letting them know how proud he was of each and every one of the them. Two, when the deputy and general saw a situation – for example, having 10 guardsmen on duty on a stretch of a city street in the pitch dark with no police car in site - action was taken to provide armed police officers close by. Both BG Klein and the Deputy Commissioner Ardomat made sure armed police officers were placed with each group of Army National Guard soldiers. This was especially confirmed in those parts of the perimeter that had no street lights.

The logistics pipeline kicked in as generators from those units on duty and from supporting elements provided enough generator power to light up the streets on the first night. Soldiers who noticed falling debris from Ground Zero that could be a potential safety hazards used chemical lights to mark them. NYPD thought this was a terrific idea so the Army issued chemical lights for their day-to-day operations.

BG Klein continued Y2K-developed relationships with all the first responding agencies which is why the New York Army National Guard and the other first responding agencies became one team in less than 72 hours. BG Klein's Y2K planning carried over to 9/11 in a successful fashion. Y2K improved administratively by having the units alert lists updated for quicker response to mobilization. The task force mobilization concept was to have units in the New York City area lined up under the 53rd Troop Command for national disasters. There was no confusion at the state headquarters. Everyone knew who was going to be in charge.

Chapter 8

Emergency Operations Center – EOC

The 53rd Troop Commander Brigadier General Klein had already received a phone call from the New York Army National Guard Adjutant General after the first plane hit. So, Gen. Klein made his way down to Ground Zero knowing that a disaster of that caliber would require the New

Command and Control

York Army National Guard to mobilize. He was still thinking the first plane crash was a freak plane accident, but a search and rescue mission was imminent.

Col. Edelman, the 53rd Troop Command Chief of Staff reflects:

"I remember it being a warm September morning without a cloud in the sky. I was in my office, behind my desk, when operations/training Sergeant Major Carl Fitje stuck his head in the door to tell me that a plane had struck one of the Twin Towers.

To be honest, I really did not think that much about it as similar events happened years ago involving the Empire State Building. But, when he came in a short time later to tell me that the second tower was just hit by another plane, I realized that something was up and it wasn't good.

Although State Headquarters had not called yet, I was in immediate contact with the commander of the 53rd Troop Command, BG Edward Klein, and other part-time members of the command. Our Emergency Operations Center [EOC] was powered up and manned. Oh yeah, I also called my wife and told her I wouldn't be coming home anytime soon, which she totally understood."

Once Col. Edelman was in direct contact with BG Klein, BG Klein said to him, "Fire up the 53rd Troop Command Emergency Operation Center. We are in command and control of a full mobilization."

We were in charge of Task Force 1 which geographically covers the New York City's area

Command and Control

Army National Guard units, and the surrounding upstate units.

Other key part-time members of headquarters had to be contacted. For instance, Col. Edelman tasked me to call Major Simon Hu, who at the time was our newest G-4 logistics officer. I knew at the time that Maj. Hu was a program analyst for Morgan Stanley. His workplace was in Building 5 of the World Trade Center.

According to Wikipedia, "Building 5 World Trade Center [5WTC] was originally a steel-framed nine-story low-rise office building built in 1970-'72 at New York City's World Trade Center. It suffered severe damage and partial collapse on its upper floors as a result of the September 11 attacks., The remaining structure was demolished by Port

Authority in December 2001, making way for reconstruction."

I called Maj. Simon Hu's home, hoping that somehow, he was not at work and would answer the phone. But his phone kept on ringing with no answer, so I was almost sure that Maj. Hu was at his workplace in that building during the attack. Maj. Hu, at the time, was an up-and-coming logistics officer; his intelligence with automation was through the roof. I worked well with him during Y2K and when preparing our units for mobilization. I was able to find Maj. Hu 20 years later and reached out to him. This is his narrative of what Sept. 11, 2001 was like for him:

"9/11 2001 was a beautiful autumn day with the clearest, bluest sky in my memory. I went to work to Morgan Stanley at the World Trade Center that morning. The subway was slow and running stop and go. I got out at Fulton Street after 9 a.m. – damn, late again. "I sensed something was unusual and police outside the station told people that a plane had hit the World Trade Center. Everyone was to turn around, get back on the subway and go home. Well, that was not going to happen – the subway had stopped running. Looking up at the WTC, I saw both towers were smoking but only saw one of the holes and thought a small plane had hit that building. Then I realized the hole was more than four stories tall. I moseyed over to 5 World Trade Center, my workplace, and this was true! A crowd was outside watching the towers burn. I found some of my co-workers, ones like me, not smart enough to run away, and we hung around swapping gossip as to what happened and waiting for instruction.

"We got the word from the management to go to Morgan Stanley's back-up site at Varick Street, so we leisurely walked there. By that time, the burning odors and black floating silts started to fill the air. Shortly after I arrived at my Morgan Stanley back-up site and was waiting, there was a low thunder rumble and someone called out, 'The tower collapsed!' That was beyond anyone's imagination. More waiting, another low rumble, the second tower collapsed too. The management informed everyone 'Go home, don't call us, we'll call you.' Out of the back-up site, I walked uptown, figuring what to do. I decided to report to an armory for duty. I walked to the 69th Armory on 25th Street. At the 69th, the unit was in the process of mobilizing. I showed up in my civilian clothes and reported for duty. I got a look over and was told to report to my own unit and that getting to 53TC of course would be a bit difficult as NYC was locked down.

"I continued to walk home in the floating silts...to 82nd Street. I changed into BDU and went to the 107th Support Group at the Park Avenue Armory. I called the Troop Command and somehow got through. I was instructed to remain at Park Avenue Armory to support on-going operation.

"I was assigned to work logistics during the nightshift, 12 hours, with an S4 sergeant who was pulling a 24-hour shift. When I arrived on September 11 in the evening for duty, I immediately began helping the nightshift crew. If I remember the situation correctly, after 9/11, we had an overabundance of resources. There were engineer units that had just come back from military training, and a massive amount of engineer equipment was lined up, ready to be used to support the 9/11 search and rescue mission. Operation wise, we were very much so in the supporting role to many civilian agencies. The NYFD and the NYPD were where most of our support was being used. One thing during the operation that does stick out in my mind is that there were lots of civilian food donations just dropped off to the Park Avenue Armory. We were told to watch out for possible terrorist poisoning in those packages where senders were unknown.

"During most of the nightshift, I answered phones, passed messages to the shift commander and sat in meetings. I was able to relieve the shift leaders who were pulling the first day's 24-hour shift duty. On September 13, after my shift, I went home and was shocked to find a voice message telling me to get back to Morgan Stanley for recovery work. I spent the next week or so pulling 20 hours a day. My day shift was for Morgan Stanley and my nights were for Uncle Sam. I probably looked pretty bad as I went to Morgan Stanley in my battle dress uniform – [BDU].

I dozed off at my desk every opportunity I could. I did have one upside though – I got a kiss from a company glamour girl and sadly, that never went anywhere."

Apparently, the evacuation of Building 5 began shortly after the North Tower was hit. The South Tower crash had deposited some remains of Flight 175's hull on the roof of WTC 5, according to the Federal Emergency Management Agency – [FEMA] report. WTC5 was severely damaged by fallout from the destruction of the towers.

Command and Control

Pictured is Maj. Simon Hu's workplace, World Trade Center Building 5 after the attack of Sept. 11, 2001. The South Tower crash deposited some remains of Flight 175's hull on the roof of WTC5, according to the Federal Emergency Management Agency – [FEMA] report.

Ron Sardanopoli

Back at the EOC, the 53rd Troop Command, everyone was relieved that Maj. Hu's delayed train ride on September 11, 2001 may have saved his life.

In the command-and-control center, Col. Edelman appointed me lead logistics team representative now that he assigned Maj. Hu to work at the Park Avenue Armory in New York City.

In the beginning, no better words can describe what this felt like other than "total chaos." In the beginning, communication was down from Ground Zero to our command center.

Certain cell phones were working. Only those cell phones that did not have the New York City area codes seemed to be working. Those New York

Command and Control

City landlines and cell phones did not work due to the crash of the Twin Towers.

My cell phone had an upstate New York area code so my phone was working. Only a few key officers and non-commissioned officers were able to call me directly with emergency supply requests. Our communications were a disaster, but when we did have an emergency logistics request on the first day, we were able to eventually deliver.

Every day at 6:30 a.m., my first phone call was with the New York Army National Guard's State Director of Logistics – [DOL]. I provided day-to-day updates about our logistics status.

Every section in the EOC had landlines. As soon as the logistics phone rang and someone picked up the receiver, it was a call requesting supplies for Ground Zero.

In the beginning, multiple calls were made by soldiers from Ground Zero asking for the same supplies that had already been requested and were in the pipeline for delivery.

At this point, there were many small cells forming at Ground Zero. They had limited communication with their counterparts that were only street corners away.

On the first day, Ground Zero was in a totally chaotic tempo. The small guard cells formed up with the bucket brigades to save lives.

In the meantime, BG Klein at Ground Zero and the 53rd Troop Command chain of command were organizing and forming their main logistics

Command and Control

and operational task force cells that those small cells could fall into to receive further instructions. Back at the EOC 53rd Troop Command, my logistics staff at the Emergency Operation Center/53rd Command Center in Valhalla, N.Y. consisted of the central property book team headed by CW4 Anthony Baldi. This team covers the breadth of the logistics and supply missions. Our property book team was able to view the on-hand balance of all our subordinate units' equipment through automation.

Our maintenance team was able to determine if the equipment such as bulldozers and cranes to move heavy debris requested for Ground Zero were serviceable, meaning "it works."

Any military piece of equipment that was serviceable and needed for this search and

rescue mission was delivered to Ground Zero.
Deliveries of bulk supplies were transported to
the Jacob Javits Center to support Ground Zero.
Our Bus transportation representative was
headed by CW4 Gerald Wieczorek, and I'm sad to
say he is no longer with us, he is deceased.
Chief Wieczorek did an outstanding job having
buses on call, ready for the next troop maneuver
directed by our Operations Officer LTC Likar. We
had parked buses in our Valhalla Armory drill
floor, ready for their next missions. Buses were
used as troop carriers, sending troops down to
Ground Zero and returning them back to their
rest and shower locations. The troops returning
from Ground Zero were covered in white silt
from head to toe due to the floating debris at
Ground Zero.

Command and Control

Donations consisted mostly of toiletry items for our troops and for the civilians. Buses transported those donations down to the Jacob Javits Center which was used as our supply center during the search and rescue mission. The Javits center also housed troops for rest and meals. My outstanding food service representative was CW4 Richard Macklin, he monitored the food availability for our soldiers at Ground Zero and also for our soldiers on duty at the Valhalla command center.

He informed me that all our units that deployed took their Meals Ready to Eat – [MREs} with them to use as their first couple of meals. Each unit's supply sergeant was able to find local diners and restaurants to provide food for their troops for the remaining time on duty. The business owners trusted the state vouchers backed by the state and FEMA funds to receive payments for their work at a later date. In an interview with BG Edward G. Klein, commander of the 53rd Troop Command and the New York Center for Military History, on October 13, 2001, BG Klein responded to a question about food for our soldiers, here is BG Klein's description "The first couple of meals were MREs and then what happened was the civilians came to our aid. There were so many donations. I mean, if you look past the devastation to check on my soldiers, there were so many donations. If you looked down the streets outside Ground Zero, it looked like a festival by day 2. McDonalds set up a booth and there was Pizza Hut, Burger King, plenty of water and coffee. It was hard to walk a city street without someone trying to offer you a sandwich. It was fantastic support."

Our 53rd Troop Command Supply Sergeant, Sergeant first Class – SFC Douglas Marcantonio, did an outstanding job collecting every state voucher and copies of purchase receipts made at ground zero. He forwarded all the receipts and financial paper work to the New York Army National Guard state office for processing so the vendors who provided services got paid.

When food and supplies needed for our troops at Ground Zero were not available in our property book inventory or at a higher source of supply, we needed to go to local vendors to provide food and supplies for our troops at certain remote locations and times. Various emergency supplies were needed for the troops who were on special missions with the NYPD to clear the surrounding buildings in case of a possible terrorist ground attack.

Master Sergeant Danny Mancuso was our motor pool supervisor and an outstanding logistics staff maintenance supervisor. MSG Mancuso, along with our state maintenance office representatives, were on top of all the maintenance concerns during this mission.

After losing our senior enlisted soldier, MSG Dominick Ciccarielli, to retirement around May, I gained an outstanding replacement to fill the outgoing master sergeant's shoes.

MSG Frank Kania fit in like a new suit, immediately getting leadership respect from his subordinate staff. He had a very knowledgeable and go-getter persona. During September 11, my staff nicknamed him "Special K" and I thought that described him perfectly.

Together we all made up the 53rd Troop Command Logistics staff.

Col. Edelman, the 53rd Troop Command Chief of Staff reflects:

"Our G-3 [operations] LTC Bodt was away at an out-of-state conference. Due to restrictions on travel, he could not be back for a few days."

While our Commander BG Klein was working to establish command and control at Ground Zero, Col. Edelman decided to use our Inspector General Joseph Likar. LTC Likar is a Vietnam veteran and was held in high regard as our inspector general. LTC Edelman reflects:

"LTC Likar, who was actually our inspector general – [IG], jumped right in and performed in a truly outstanding manner. LTC Liker had a calm demeanor which allowed him and his staff to perform successfully in a very stressful environment. The commands effective performance during those early days after September 11 was the result, to a great degree, of his noteworthy efforts."

I was able to find and reconnect with Lieutenant Colonel [Ret.] Likar. He shares his memory while serving as the G-3 operations officer for the 53rd Troop Command for this 9/11 mission.

LTC Liker's narrative:

"The morning of September 11 began normally. At approximately 9:30, I went to the dining hall for coffee. While there, the newscasters were reporting on a plane that just flew into one of the towers of the World Trade Center. There was much speculation regarding the crash. Perhaps the pilot was lost or he could not see the tower. While this debate continued, a second plane flew into the second tower.

I then went to my quarters to pick up my go bag and headed for the armory in Valhalla, N.Y., about 50 miles from where I lived. U.S. 9 was okay to travel until I got to Annville Circle. Traffic was snarled and I could see the smoke from the fires in New York City.

I arrived at the armory after an hour and a half drive.

I reported to Col. Robert Edelman, the Chief of Staff. I was informed that I was the first M-Day soldier – traditional soldier – to report and I was to be the G-3 operations officer initially.

I accepted the assignment and immediately went to open the Emergency Operations Center. It was totally chaotic. To get a handle on things, I issued several operation orders, instructing subordinate units to continue to assemble at Home Station [HS] but remain until called up.

Not knowing how many funds were being allocated for the emergency, I must be prudent. While the Division of Military and Naval Affairs [DMNA] operations officer, Director of Training was in Washington, D.C. during the initial events, no guidance from the state was had for several hours. I assessed the situation and determined transportation was needed to move the donations from the Javits Center to warehouses

procured for that purpose. Engineers were needed to move debris from Ground Zero and maintenance to keep it all operational. After issuing the required orders, I received a call from the director of training requesting a status update, which I gave him. He asked why weapons and ammunition were not issued and accompanied the soldiers to NYC. I informed him that we did not have "Posse Comitatus authority"
*

[*For non-military readers, the Posse Comitatus Act is a United States federal law signed on June 18, 1878 by Pres. Rutherford B. Hayes which limits the powers of the federal government in the use of federal military personnel to enforce domestic policies within the United States. In other words, no weapons were authorized to be

used for this mission.] LTC Likar's narrative continued, "While all military assets of NY State were being used to include the NY Guard, the state militia, every unit at or near Ground Zero had a liaison officer assigned. The 107th Corps Support group, based in NYC, was one of the initial units to be deployed. The headquarters deployed soldiers to Ground Zero to assist in recovery operations. While [there was] a request from the FDNY to have soldiers hose off the boots of the firemen as they exited Ground Zero, if requested the soldiers could manage the decontamination station, but washing off boots was not in our job description and I disapproved the mission. Shortly after disapproving the mission, I received a call from the 107th Corps Support S-3 operations officer asking why his soldiers were cleaning the boots of firemen. I informed him the request was denied and I would investigate it. I had found the NYG officer who approved the mission after it was disapproved. I immediately called the officer and asked why he approved it. He said he approved all requests from NYPD or NYFD, at which point I told him to leave. After what felt like an eternity, the EOC had an Air Force Col. Scuttina from the 106th Air Rescue Wing. My team and I were finally relieved of duty for at least eight hours to get cleaned up and rested."

I was also fortunate enough to make contact with LTC [Ret.] Likar's staff operations NCO, Master Sergeant [Ret.] Thomas Lambert. Here is MSG Lambert's narrative:

Ron Sardanopoli

"On the morning of September 11, 2001, SGM Fitje and myself were preparing for a training conference at the 53rd Troop Command Headquarters. Shortly before 9 a.m., word was spreading around the office that a small plane had crashed into one of the towers at the World Trade Center. We turned on the TV to see what we could find out. What we saw was news coverage showing the crash site, and the news being reported was sketchy at best. People were trying to figure out what had just happened.

"Shortly thereafter we learned of a second plane crashing into the South Tower. At that moment SGM Fitje and I realized that this was no coincidence and made the decision to open the EOC located on the ground level of our headquarters.

Command and Control

The EOC is a turnkey operations center equipped with computers, phones and tools to conduct business in such emergencies. In a relatively short period of time, all areas of Operations, Logistics and Personnel were up and running. The first day was an emotional one. As I drove home that day after midnight, tears came to my eyes seeing all of the American flags being displayed in front of people's homes. I continued to work 12-hour shifts for the next 15 days. It was amazing to see the dedication and professionalism being displayed by all of the members of the New York Army National Guard. I worked directly for LTC Joe Likar who had the ability and talent to make a difficult situation look easy."

At the 53rd Troop Command Center, there was lots of screaming and yelling in this EOC room.

Ron Sardanopoli

Total chaos! Everyone was shouting about what they heard was needed at Ground Zero.

My transportation officer was able to marshal buses at the Valhalla Armory to pick up and deliver donations collected by the local fire departments for our troops down at Ground Zero.

Our supply team was finding the various equipment needed; many units that were mobilized already had generators of all sizes to begin helping in the search and rescue. Receiving supply requests and transportation requests was difficult, mostly because communication was extremely weak in the early days of this mission. So, for the first 48 to 72 hours, the same soldiers who were called out to duty both at Ground Zero and the command center were not getting the needed rest. From the bucket brigades at Ground Zero to the planners and shakers at the command center, the mindset for everyone was to save lives.

At the command center, the voice noise sounded louder than the stock exchange after the opening bell rings. Sometimes the noise was disruptive because people wanted to be heard over the loud noise. It seemed at times like boarder line pandemonium with yelling across the room from the G-1 operations section and the G-3 personnel section, and the G-4 logistics section.

I got my clipboard and soldiers surrounded me, giving me their supply requests received from Ground Zero. Voices coming from all directions saying,

"Chief, we need generators for nighttime lighting, light sets, engineer equipment to move the debris from the destroyed WTC buildings" or "We need tents for the troops to rest overnight in local parks." And the requests for supplies kept coming.

Some of those requests were found in our subordinate unit's property listings belonging to our subordinate units. Sometimes the ground soldiers are not aware of all the equipment they own. Not realizing the problem of not having communications within themselves was adding to the chaos.

A request for Army tents came to my desk the first day. They needed tents as a temporary hold area for human body parts. The collection of body parts was needed to identify people who perished in the attack by checking the DNA. An estimated 2,753 people were killed at the World Trade Center site. Just 293 bodies were found intact. There was a total of 21,900 body parts/pieces that were recovered from the debris.

It comes out to about 60% of the victims had been identified. The remains of 1,113 people were unidentified, despite the costliest forensic investigation – at $80 million-plus – in U.S. history.

Many doctors and nurses from the local hospitals volunteered for the collection of body parts. The painstaking efforts for those involved in this mission must still be banded in their memory banks.

Days after the attack, New York Mayor Rudy Giuliani announced that there was little hope of finding more survivors, but pledged that, "the Office of the Chief Medical Examiner [OCME] would do whatever it took to identify the source of every single human remain recovered from the WTC, no matter how small."

There are many legal matters that erupt with our soldiers as a result of Sept. 11. Our attorney, Judge Advocate General – JAG Col. Thomas Principe, was also being contacted.

Col. Principle was assigned to our headquarters for legal matters. He knew the military for more than 27 years during this call-up. And he knew the law, on both the military and civilian sides. He understood what it means to be a service member and a civilian lawyer. He had been multi-tasking to assist our primary staff as an attorney for a number of military legal matters involving our soldiers, and yet held a position as a civilian attorney and was always helping people. Col. Principe was an outstanding asset for our soldiers, our staff and the New York Army National Guard.

I was able to make contact with Col. Principe and am grateful he had the time to provide me with his narrative of how Sept. 11, 2001 went for him:

"September 11, 2001 began for me on the day before because 9/10 pre-determined my movements on 9/11. On September 10, 2001, I had been in the U.S. Army, either Army Reserve or U.S. Army National Guard for 27 years.

Ron Sardanopoli

"On September 10, 2001, I had also been a lawyer for 27 years. My "civilian" job was being a partner in the law firm of Kramer, Dolloff, Livingston & Moore, located in the Woolworth Building which, by the following day, September 11, would lie within the Ground Zero perimeter. On the morning of September 10, I was assisting a client of our firm, a profoundly disabled young woman who had suffered severe injuries from a "slip of the knife" during spinal surgery. Due to her injuries, this young woman was paralyzed on one side of her body and also had an additional condition wherein the slightest touch to the skin on the affected side of her body caused terrible pain. Not only was her ability to move around severely compromised from these injuries, but she was also in her fifth month of pregnancy. Her injuries were such that her obstetrician was unsure how her pregnancy would progress and how her labor might be complicated by her paralysis. For many reasons, my client was in a delicate condition. This young client lived in Florida but had traveled to the New York area where she was staying with her brother in Westchester so she could testify at an Examination Before Trial [EBT]. In that situation, a person is sworn to tell the truth as if they are in court and their testimony is taken down by a court reporter.

"This EBT was taking place in our firm's offices on the 45th floor of the Woolworth Building. The RBT, her sworn testimony, went on all day in our office with the attorney for the defendant doctor who had operate on her and the attorney for the hospital where the operation took place asking question after question, relentlessly. When it was nearing 5 p.m., the defense attorney asked for the client to be brought back for more questioning the following day, September 11. I said that I would not want her to go through the struggle of going to Westchester that night and coming back to the office in the morning. If the court reporter could stay and continue recording the testimony, I would like everyone to stay until the questioning was finished so that [the client] would not need to return to our office. The court reporter said she could stay and both defense attorneys agreed that they could stay, so the EBT continued until about 7:30 p.m. when my client could leave without needing to return. I was then given an assignment for the next day which

Command and Control

would be on Long Island where I resided, to appear in court at 1 p.m. On the morning of September 11, 2001, a few minutes before 9 a.m., our home telephone rang. It was our neighbor asking my wife, "Where is your husband?" because she knew I worked in Lower Manhattan. My wife replied that I was at home with an assignment on Long Island that day. Turn on your television, a plane just flew into the World Trade Center. We turned on the television and saw the second airliner fly into the World Trade Center South Tower at 9:30 a.m. in real time. After grappling with what we had just seen, I decided that I should call headquarters of the 53rd Troop Command in Valhalla, New York to ask how I was needed for National Guard service. Phone service was disrupted in various ways and the Troop Command Headquarters telephone

was always busy. After constant re-dialing, the

telephone was answered and Chief of Staff

[second in command under BG Edward Klein,

Commander] Col. Robert Edelman [now Brigadier

General Ret.] said two words: "Come in." I put on

my uniform, got into my civilian vehicle and

began the drive to the 53rd Troop Command

Headquarters in Valhalla, New York. The roads

had been cleared and closed by this time; mine

was the only car moving. Every roadblock allowed

me passage because 1.) I was wearing my

uniform and 2.) I was driving away from

Manhattan instead of toward it. Troop Command

Headquarters was grappling with severe

communication problems. The Trade Center

towers had been an enormous hub for wireless

communication and all cell phone service was cancelled for miles around. As a result, landlines were jammed with incoming calls and it was nearly impossible to make outgoing calls. Many officers and troops, including commanders, were isolated from headquarters.

Upon arrival in Valhalla on the afternoon of 9/11, I had a lot on my mind. It was decided that there would be a briefing in Valhalla at 7 a.m. each morning. I had been hoping to go to the Park Avenue Armory [Park Avenue] at 643 Park Ave. in Manhattan because I was also the JAG officer for the 107th Support Group, ["the 107th"], commanded by Col. [now Maj. Gen. Ret.] Stephen R. Seiter, headquartered at Park Avenue. Because time was too short, with the comprehensive traffic shut-down, to try to get to

Park Avenue, I decided to stay in Valhalla overnight to be present for the 7 a.m. briefing on September 12, 2001. I had brought my military sleeping bag and my military cot in the car with me and I slept by my desk in a small partitioned cubicle in the Valhalla office area. Personnel all around me were working through the night so sleep was fitful, but necessary.

During the 7 a.m. briefing on September 12, 2001, it was reviewed which troops had been deployed to which locations. Following the briefing, I drove to the 107th at the Park Avenue Armory and from Park Avenue to Ground Zero to visit the 53rd Troop Command troops. Ground Zero was like a "nuclear winter," to borrow the words of the commander of the 101st Cavalry, stationed in Staten Island, N.Y. The high temperature reached 77 degrees F on September 12. It was hot in our uniforms, hot wearing our facemasks, and difficult to breathe once the facemask, the face and the uniform became coated with the Ground Zero "dust." The smoke, the smell and the silt were overwhelming and seemed suffocating.

The sun was shining, but not within the newly-designated Ground Zero perimeter which was a thick, murky haze with "the Pit" where the Trade Center towers had fallen, belching massive clouds of blinding smoke that would continue for 100 days.

Into the belching furnace marched our troops from the nearest point of entry at Battery Park."

Chapter 9

Controlled Chaos

Forty-eight to 72 hours after the attack, there
was a sudden, almost magical collaboration of
team members. Commanders and soldiers
established processes and then set them in stone
at Ground Zero. Missions were created and
completed in record times compared to the first
couple of days, and there was quick turnaround

on most requests at Ground Zero. It ended the pandemonium and total chaos that our soldiers were dealing with both at Ground Zero and the 53rd Troop Command Center in Valhalla, New York.

Why did this happen?

I remember clearly why this happened. Being the 53rd Troop Commands senior logistics coordinator for this national disaster, while I was working at the 53rd Command Center [EOC], I was being bombarded with supply requests from people wanting supplies at Ground Zero. The noise level at the command center was through the roof. Everyone was trying to relay their important messages to others.

Then came into our command center Captain Farrier. At a glance, I captured Cpt. Farrier trying to catch my attention by locking eye contact to make sure she was being heard. She explained what she could do to help with our communication problem between our soldiers at Ground Zero and our command center.

Before I go on to Cpt. Farrier's remarkable, selfless actions, I'll share my thoughts about the importance of communication at a command-and-control center.

"Command is what commanders do. They do it with communication. Command and control are how they do it. Those are the simple facts about the nature of military leadership – command and control are always used in conjunction with each other and communication is key."

It was the efforts of one signal officer soldier who brought in the element of command and control. She took it upon herself to fix our communication problem.

Cpt. Kim Farrier was the commander of Company C 230th Signal Battalion and made an amazing decision that improved our communications problem. She was able to make a connection with her civilian job to have them donate Nextel field-style phones to key officers and enlisted personnel in the New York Army National Guard. These phones allowed us to communicate amongst ourselves and with state agencies. These field phones were able to work with a wireless signal.

Command and Control

I was able to catch up with [now] Lieutenant Colonel [Ret.] Kim Farrier and she gave me a narrative about her miraculous accomplishment:

"I was in Valhalla, New York by around noon that day. My rank in 2001 was captain. I was Company Commander of C Company 230th Signal Battalion out of Orangeburg, New York. I was assigned there by the commander of the 53rd Troop Command. I had access to Nextel Corporation as a result of the working relationship I had with them. My working relationship with Nextel began during my coordination of communications for the National Veterans Wheelchair Games for the Department of Veterans Affairs in July 2001. I had 250 walkie talkie devises, complete with banks of battery chargers and spare batteries within 24 hours. They were fully charged with a phone directory and distribution plan in 36 hours. My distribution plan went into effect immediately. All devises were distributed to command elements within 48 hours, and by the evening shift change on September 12, 2001, the 53rd Troop Command had comprehensive command and control due to those Nextel devises. They worked both as push-to-talk as well as a regular cell phone. The key was their total interoperability with NYPD as well as the NYFD and other first responders."

After Cpt. Farrier forwarded me her narrative, she sent me this short message: She wanted to let me know that, "God was on our side."

Command and Control

Once our communication opened up from Ground Zero to our command center due to Cpt. Farrier's Nextel phone devises, I whispered, "Thank You, God."

The severe communication problem that the collapse of the Trade Center towers caused was improved. Once we were able to communicate with the new Nextel devises, mission requests became easier to complete. As LTC Farrier captured it in her narrative, "the 53rd Troop Command had comprehensive command and control due to those Nextel devises." Indeed, we did! My logistics communications with the supply chain of command improved. I was in immediate contact with the specific individuals who needed supplies at Ground Zero, and the people in the supply chain who could issue those supplies. The flow of communication became open to our entire primary staff at the 53rd Troop Command's Emergency Operation Center.

That included all representatives at Task Force 1 at the Park Avenue Armory, our logistics forward in New York City, and also with Task Force 1 at Battery Park, in New York City our operational forward. All supply requests from Ground Zero were received using the Nextel devices to our operations officer at the

53rd EOC, LTC Liker, 53rd Troop Command G-3. A G-3 staff member walked the mission over to our logistics section. The logistics section wrote the mission on our mission board.

Mission requests were flowing in. For example, there were requests for ponchos to deal with rainy days, cots for soldiers to sleep on overnight

Command and Control

at various facilities, generators, and light sets for 1st responders to work the night shift at ground zero, and the perimeter defense, engineers' equipment for the removal of debris, tents for cells operating in Battery Park.

I remember a G-3 staff member shouting out to me, "Chief, we need to increase the count on a lunch meal for our special guests." I yelled back, "What special guests?" He responded, "Joe Torre and the New York Yankees."

I remember that weeks later the local news channel gave credit to the New York Yankees for chipping in to help our first responders. The news covered Bernie Williams and Derek Jeter and other Yankee players who helped our soldiers off-load supplies at the Javits Center.

Ron Sardanopoli

The Javits Center, where our bulk supplies were kept, was 1.2 miles from Ground Zero. Once the supplies reached the Jacob Javits Center, the mission was given to the 107th Corps Support Group Task Force 1 [forward]. The 107th Corps Support tasked the 206 Corps Support Battalion and the 369th Corps Support Battalion [Harlem Hellfighters] to transport the supplies needed to Ground Zero.

Every day at the command center in Valhalla, N.Y., at 6:30 a.m., I briefed our director of logistics – DOL – at New York State Headquarters, Latham, N.Y., on the current status of our logistic missions.

At 7 a.m., I along with others primary staff members briefed deputy commander and our Chief of Staff at our 53rd Troop Command Center

Command and Control

Headquarters on the overall status of our logistics, manpower, and operations at Ground Zero. The briefings were conducted every morning and evening when the 12-hour shift changed.

Our Commander BG Klein reflects: "Colonel James Scuttina, Vice Wing Commander at Headquarters 105th Rescue Wing, was in charge of the day shift, and Col. Paul Genereux was in charge of the night shift. They were both given deputy commander designation and authority. Col. Robert Edelman was the 53rd Troop Command Chief of Staff and primary advisor to both Col. Scuttina and Col. Genereux. Col. Edelman's institutional knowledge of how the National Guard works at the state level was invaluable to all the senior leaders at the 53rd

Troop Command."

Command and Control

Pictured at the EOC/53rd Troop Command Center, Valhalla, N.Y., [center] BG Klein, Commander 53rd Troop Command is being briefed by the night shift Deputy Commander [Left] Col. Genereux, while the 53rd Troop Command Chief of Staff [Right] Col. Robert Edelman, listens in.

In addition to having those Nextel devises that offered a great deal of help to organize our daytime shift, Deputy Commander

Ron Sardanopoli

Col. Scuttina brought with him about 10 or 12 of his staff members to fill in and help our very thin staff to help manage both day and night shifts. When Col. Scuttina and his staff members joined our staff, relief was written on the faces of the 53rd Troop Command's primary staff. Many of the 1st responder EOC staff members who worked 36 to 48 hours [no rest] on September 11, and 12 were able to get their needed rest.

We all began functioning at a controlled but stressful work pace like well-oiled and seasoned Army National Guard soldiers are trained to do. Col. Robert Edelman reflects:

"I recollect the tremendous support we received from the 106th Rescue Wing Air National Guard - ANG from Long Island, New York. Led by Colonel Scuttina, a group of about a dozen

Command and Control

soldiers, a mixture of officers and enlisted noncommissioned officers – NCOs – were sent to our Valhalla command center to supplement the command's relatively small staff. Each of them performed in a highly professional manner and made our ability to accomplish assigned missions a little less difficult. It also allowed us to run an effective and responsive 24-hour operation."

A state headquarters' director of logistics – DOL – representative was relocated from upstate in Latham, N.Y. to our command-and-control center in Valhalla to work alongside my logistics staff. When a supply request came through our supply chain and we could not fill it, the state DOL representative took immediate action to fill that request. If the DOL could not satisfy supply requests within the New York State inventory, he went further up the supply chain to fill it.

The DOL contacted the DOL at the National Guard Bureau in Washington for those resources. Washington's DOL checked the Army National Guard units within the United States starting with those units located in the tri-state area to fill the request.

For example, when the request for additional outdoor tents for temporarily storing human body parts, Task Force 1 , 53rd Troop Command subordinate units in the State of New York could not fill that request.

The DOL was able to get those tents from another state. I received a phone call soon after we submitted our request to the DOL. That request for tents needed for the human body parts was filled by the Connecticut Army National Guard.

In a phone conversation, the Connecticut National Guard representative asked me, "Chief Sardanopoli, where do you want these tents to be delivered?" I was so impressed with the quick turn-around. The urgency of need for emergency supplies during the aftermath of this terrorist attack was critical.

All of the Army National Guards located outside the State of New York had our backs during this national disaster. We were trained to work the supply chain during combat missions and national disasters. But when you actually get to see it work so quickly and smoothly during a live mission like 9/11, there is a feeling of unbelievable pride because of the work accomplished by my logistics team and the Army supply chain [pipeline].

With our new Nextel wireless phones distributed at Ground Zero, our commander, BG Klein, was able to contact all the small cells that formed on the first day, and have them join the command structure of the 53rd Troop Command, Task Force 1. The Park Avenue Armory became Task Force 1 forward, headed up by Col. Steven Seiter who was the commander of the 107th Corps Support Group. Ground Zero was 3.5 miles away from the Park Avenue Armory. This was where BG Klein moved into on day 1 to set up a forward Tactical Operation Center – TOC. This is where the general spent most of his time, to be close to his deployed subordinate commanders and soldiers at Ground Zero.

Command and Control

Task Force 1 [forward] [the Park Avenue Armory], also gave BG Klein access to the New York City Office of Emergency Management and its officials.

As Task Force 1 [forward] became overwhelmed with the number of soldiers reporting in to be given their maneuver assignments, BG Klein, together with his subordinate commanders, decided that this mission needed to spread out. A second headquarters, under the leadership of Col. Ray Doyle, located at Battery Park, Lower Manhattan, was established. The Park Avenue Armory, Task Force 1, became the [logistical forward] headquarters. The Battery Park Lower Manhattan became the Task Force 1 [operational forward] headquarters, located 0.7 miles from Ground Zero.

Both of these headquarters reported to the EOC, 53rd Troop Command Center Headquarters in Valhalla, New York.

Command and Control

Pictured are New York Army National Guard soldiers marching from Battery Park, Task Force 1 [Operational forward], in Lower Manhattan, 0.7 miles from Ground Zero.

Ron Sardanopoli

The remarkably strong leadership style BG Klein provided to lead the 53rd Troop Command, Task Force 1, will never be forgotten. Here is a reflection given to me by our Chief of Staff Col. Robert Edelman:

"I can recall what a strong leader General Klein was, making one smart decision after another. Although his headquarters was in Valhalla, N.Y., he immediately set up a mini-Emergency Operation Center at the Park Avenue Armory, Task Force 1, which was a lot closer to Ground Zero.

I can remember the General taking many strong stands against requests by state headquarters. Being closer to his commanders and enlisted soldiers at Ground Zero, he had a better feel for what missions had to be accomplished and what units were required to do the job."

As I collected everyone's narratives, I was able to put together more events and strategies used at Ground Zero. These narratives and interviews with first responders validate the exceptional professionalism the Army National Guard provides to our communities during national disasters.

Chapter 10

Clean Up

The balance of the first two weeks of duty at Ground Zero was dedicated to cleaning up the debris from the collapsed buildings, and continuing the search and rescue for bodies and body parts for DNA accountability.

The possibility of a terrorist ground attack at Ground Zero was still looming in the Army National Guard planning and executing stages.

The Army National Guard and New York Police officers were extremely anxious about the idea of a ground attack.

BG Klein and the NYPD together executed a perimeter defense and the clearing of buildings around Ground Zero. Those initial preventative measures eventually mitigated the thought of any hostile actions.

The 53rd Troop Command Judge Advocate General – JAG – at the time, Col. Principe, reflects back about his time serving at Ground Zero the first two weeks. Here is the now Brigadier General [R] Thomas J. Principe's narrative:

"Into Ground Zero marched our 53rd Troop Command officers and troops on September 12, 2001. They had no communication capability until our personnel who happened to work for various telephone service providers in their civilian jobs were able to establish a wireless network and issue Motorola "field type" telephones which could attract a wireless signal. As a JAG officer, I could not offer them a place to rest or a dust-free environment, but I could offer to relieve them of some of the problems which assail most people: legal problems, court appearances, minor discipline problems, civilian employment problems, domestic relations issues, and other problems which became major thorns in their minds as they served their lonely duty. I adjourned their court appearances and civilian employers who were threatening to fire them for not showing up at their "regular" jobs.

The problems could crop up for different officers or soldiers on any day, and I wanted to show that I was supporting their service and that I was there to help them. I went to Park Avenue, Ground Zero and the Javits Center, where they were sleeping, every day. I passed out hundreds of my business cards to let them know I was there for them and legal assistance was available. It was not that I thought the officers and soldiers might leave their posts. It was that they were subjected to huge conflicts in that hostile environment. If there were more terrorist threats, shouldn't they be home defending their families? If they didn't know when they would get their National Guard pay, how could they pay their rent and buy groceries for their families? If the economy collapsed, what would happen to their civilian jobs?

The Ground Zero environment required vigilance. From September 12 onward, the flow of people reversed. Instead of running away from Ground Zero, there were well-wishers and volunteers hiking to Ground Zero, and people wearing uniforms of all types showing up at the armories to volunteer their services.

This was an overwhelming show of patriotism and Samaritans. But, at that time, there was enormous concern that there might be terrorists masquerading as volunteers and perhaps they might strike at the armories.

All National Guard personnel who were going to Ground Zero were issued official badges to display or they would not be allowed to enter the

perimeter whether or not they were in uniform.

No civilians were to be allowed to enter the

perimeter unless they had abundant

identification and relevant reasons to be there.

Command and Control

Above red "First responder" Ground Zero ID badge and subsequent blue deployment ID badge. Below, Col. [now BG Ret.] Thomas J. Principe in front of the "pile" wearing a respirator mask during 9/11 first responder deployment Sept. 11 – Sept. 24, 2001.

Ron Sardanopoli

The Ground Zero pit, where the towers had fallen and which was burning, and the Ground Zero "pile," where the rubble and building portions had heaped up after falling, were swarming with NYPD, NYFD and other rescue workers. There was a line of workers trying to clear the rubble where they literally passed buckets of ash and rubble from hand to hand down a line to remove substance from the pit.

There was tremendous concern that there might be too many workers in the pit and the weight of the workers alone might cause another collapse into the pit and the fire. Large equipment was not brought in for some time due to the instability of the pit, and the concern for recovering survivors or the bodies of the lost.

Command and Control

According to www.history.com/topics/21st-century/ground=zero "The work was so dangerous that many firefighters and police officers wrote their names and phone numbers on their forearms in case they fell into the hole or were crushed." The air quality was extremely poor down at Ground Zero. The dust, ranging in particle size, was a mixture of crushed concrete, gypsum and synthetic fibers. The high concentration of silt was deposited in the airways of the head and lungs of rescue and recovery workers, clean-up workers, residents and office workers."

The Army National Guard soldiers were issued protective masks and were told to wear them while on duty in and around Ground Zero.

Ron Sardanopoli

Here is a reflection from Col. Edelman, the 53rd Troop Command Chief of Staff:
"I can clearly remember visiting the site at Ground Zero and meeting with our units who were early responders, and discussing with them the merits of wearing their protective masks despite the city's claim that the air quality at Ground Zero was safe to breathe."

With the endless hours our soldiers at the 53rd Troop Command put into the first two weeks, the State Adjutant General ordered a transfer of the 42nd Infantry Division Headquarters to be in Command and Control. Many of our soldiers who had come on duty had just returned from Fort Polk, Louisiana where they attended the Joint readiness Training Center – JRTC training. JRTC is

Command and Control

where our soldiers learn the real pre-deployment training scenarios in all aspects of armed conflict. Also, our soldiers were traditional Army National Guard soldiers and it was important to get them back to their civilian jobs so they could get their family's lives back in order.

BG Klein and the 53rd Troop Command primary staff needed to get back to preparing its subordinate units ready for overseas deployments.

Chapter 11

Never Forget

While New York City got the order from Mayor
Giuliani to run out from the island of Manhattan
after the terrorist attacks, firefighters hugged
each other good-bye as they went up those
stairwells.

Command and Control

Police officers ran to Ground Zero when civilians ran away from it.

Soldiers' families already knew the drill – their soldier was running to Ground Zero to save lives.

Soldiers lived by these three hallowed words: duty, honor and country.

At Ground Zero, our soldiers led honorably and demonstrated excellence while performing their duties during their search and rescue missions.

The remaining essential workers, and especially those volunteers who were not invited to help in the search and rescue mission, they showed up just because they have thick skin. The United States of America appreciated your selfless service, your integrity and your courage.

Time plays a role with emotions.

Ron Sardanopoli

After 20 years, those attacks have little emotional significance to a huge portion of our population. Millions of American youth are too young to absorb the significance of the attacks. And nearly 20 million immigrants have legally come into the United States since 9/11. I say this about our immigrants because not having been a part of our society when 9/11 occurred, their emotional resonance is not the same.

To the citizen who did have a connection to this brutal attack, I ask that you never forget.

And even to those who have little emotional connection to 9/11 because they were not born yet or were not citizens 20 years ago, there is still an obligation to that memory and to respect, with gratitude, those 2,997 souls who died. That includes 343 firefighters, 23 New York City police officers, 37 Port Authority officers and 55 military personnel.

I will never forget. It's deep inside me. Honoring the dead, the police, the firefighters, EMTs, soldiers, chaplains, co-workers, the heroes on the four hijacked planes...some almost confronted certain death to save others. To those that gave the ultimate sacrifice to save others they all deserve the ultimate praise for our freedom.

There were many soldiers who reported to the search and rescue mission on that first day under the command-and-control leadership of the 53rd Troop Command. These soldiers were challenged to the extreme, they learned so much about themselves. Its already imbedded in their mindset. They are willing to give the ultimate sacrifice, when you're willing to tackle a job or a task or a mission, having this mindset, amazing things happen because they are fearless. While the citizens of New York City were running away from this tragedy, our soldiers were running to Ground Zero to save lives.

Epilogue

Now more than ever, the guardsmen were being asked to do more, both domestically and abroad. Today there are nearly 470,000 citizen soldiers and airmen comprising the Army and Air National Guard in 54 states, territories and the District of Columbia, spanning more than 3,300 American communities. Our citizen soldiers comprised of both male and female are physically and mentally tough patriots.

In my story, "Command and Control," I hope I was able to transparently describe the commitment our guardsmen and women make. That commitment is a combination of the drive they have within them, the desire to help those in need and a passion to be a keeper of the American dream. As one patriot soldier leaves, another patriot soldier is ready to fill his or her shoes.

These following patriot soldiers were first responders on 9/11 and some were contributors to my story, "Command and Control." Some of these soldiers were brevetted to the next higher rank as a reward by the New York State Army

National Guard – NYARNG and entered the NYARNG retired list.

These following military first responders volunteered their remembrances of the first horrific day and the days that followed. Because I was working at the 53rd Troop Command Operation Center on 9/11, I was unable to write about these terrorist attack events at Ground Zero without the input of these soldiers. With their narratives and interviews I was able to put the puzzle together to capture the total experience for [Command and Control].

Some of these officers and enlisted soldiers took us down to Ground Zero, Task Force 1[EOC], Task Force 1 [logistics forward], and Task Force 1 [operational forward], and the Javits Center to describe their experience. They include Maj. Gen.

Command and Control

[Ret.] Edward G. Klein, BG [Ret.] Robert M. Edelman, BG [Ret]. Thomas J. Principe, Lt. Col. [Ret.] Joseph Likar, Lt. Col. [Ret.] Kim Farrier, MSG [Ret.] Donald Tucciariello, MSG [Ret.] Thomas Lambert and MSG [Ret.] Joe Grado. Without the input from these soldiers and their narratives, my description of many strategic maneuvers and events captured at Ground Zero would not be possible.

All of MG [Ret.] Edward G. Klein's actions described in "Command and Control" are documented in the United States Army Center of Military History. BG Klein's input and his historical interview document on Oct. 13, 2001, just a couple weeks after his end of duty, became an excellent resource document that helped lay the groundwork at Ground Zero for, "Command and Control."

This became an excellent resource helping me put together the various chain of events that took place after the attack.

My contributors to "Command and Control" were:

Maj. Gen. [Ret.] Edward G, Klein who organized, supervised and coordinated all military support at Ground Zero from Sept. 11, 2001 until the end of his assignment. MG [R] Klein put together an exemplary military career. After leaving the commander's position of the 53rd Troop Command, he was promoted to commanding general of the New York Army National Guard on Jan. 24, 2002.

Command and Control

Upon retiring, BG Klein [one star] was brevetted to a major general [two stars]. Today, MG [R] Klein is enjoying his golden years in his forever home in sunny Florida. During retirement, he continues to lead, and is currently sitting as the Governor's Chairman of the Board for Squadron A Association in New York City. This association has more than 600 veterans and businessmen and was founded on April 2, 1889.

During the annual 9/11 remembrance season, he is invited to be a guest speaker at various events in rooms filled with patriots including veterans and businessmen and women.

Brigadier General [Ret.] Robert M. Edelman was a dynamic chief of staff. He knew how to stay calm, composed and ready to do what was necessary, especially in the face of adversity or crisis. Upon retirement, he was brevetted to the rank of brigadier general [one star] for his exemplary work as chief of staff. BG Edelman recently retired from the Syosset School District, Syosset, New York, where he worked for 16 years. He is enjoying his golden years with his spouse, his son, his daughter-in-law and granddaughter. Every now and then, you can find the General on the golf course. If you happen to run into him, ask him about the witnessed hole-in-one that he scored. He loves to tell that story.

Brigadier General [Ret.] Thomas J. Principe was the 53rd Troop Command Judge Advocate General – JAG. We heard from BG Principe in his narratives about the legal support

Command and Control

he brought to all our troops in the 53rd Troop

Command. His caring approach for our soldiers'

bleeds through every word in his

narratives. Upon retirement, he was brevetted to

the rank of Brigadier General [one star] because

of his exemplary legal support to our soldiers. He

is still working as a civilian attorney today.

Colonel – COL [Ret] Jacqueline Russel –[G-1]

Manpower/Administration officer was promoted

to the new rank of full bird colonel and her new

assignment became chief of staff, 53rd Troop

Command. Col. Russel became the first female

chief of staff for the 53rd Troop Command and the

first female chief of staff in the New York Army

National Guard. She will forever be known as the

first female Chief of Staff in the New York Army National Guard history, what an amazing honor. Col. Russel is enjoying retirement in her hometown of Redding, Connecticut.

Lieutenant Colonel - LTC [Ret.] Andrew Leiter – liaison officer New York Army National Guard – was stationed near Ground Zero at Pier 92, after Building 7 World Trade Center was demolished, New York City's Emergency Management Office with more than 150 other agencies.
He relayed missions to BG Klein and the 53rd Troop Command's Command Center. All maneuver missions that were relayed were approved by MG Klein and came from the NYPD or the NYFD.

Command and Control

Today Col. Leiter is a real estate attorney and has been a residential and commercial developer in New York City since 1979.

Lieutenant Colonel – LTC [Ret.] Joe Likar is a Vietnam veteran, and an Army inspector general – IG – who filled in as the 53rd Troop Command [G-3] operations officer on 9/11. He received accolades for a job well done from the 53rd Troop Command, commander. Chief of Staff and primary staff members. LTC Likar is enjoying his golden years living in North Carolina.

Lieutenant Colonel - LTC [Ret.] William Bodt [G-3] Operations Officer 53rd Troop Command who never stopped his military aid to civil authority. After retirement LTC [Ret.] Bodt became the operations and planning officer at the United States Department of Defense – DOD.

Lieutenant Colonel – LTC [Ret.] Kim Farrier, the signal officer, took it upon herself to have her civilian job donate Nextel wireless phones. After 48-72 hours, we had open communication from Ground Zero to the fire and police agencies and our 53rd Troop Command Center. A superior effort that improved our communications and support to our troops. LTC Farrier is still employed as she has more selfless service to give to others.

Master Sergeant – MSG [Ret.] Donald Tucciariello, the operation sergeant for the 1st Bn 53rd Troop Command, after notifying his military

Command and Control

police companies and 101 Signal Battalion to report for duty for a search and rescue mission at Ground Zero, felt he needed to do more. MSG Tucciariello charged down to Ground Zero to scout out the intelligence for the next move for his soldiers. MSG Tucciariello with the Military Police Companies and 101 Signal Company were needed beyond their initial call for duty, and helped at ground zero for months after.

Today MSG Tucciariello is enjoying his golden years traveling with his spouse and enjoying his time with his children and grandchildren.

Master Sergeant- MSG [Ret.] Joe Grado, the maintenance shop foreman who got his activation orders, fueled up his military vehicle and charged to his duty station to help alert the soldiers of his subordinate maintenance companies. Then he jumped in his vehicle and charged down to Ground Zero. Noticing everyone running off the island, he and hundreds of first responders were charging to Ground Zero. MSG Grado recently retired from the Board of Education, transportation section. He is enjoying his golden years in Jackson, New Jersey with his family and grandchildren.

Master Sergeant – MSG [Ret.] Thomas Lambert who was the 53rd Troop Command operations NCO was working at the 53rd Troop Command emergency operation center assisting LTC Likar. He is a retired NYPD officer. He came on active duty with the Army National Guard soon after retiring from the NYPD. MSG Lambert is

Command and Control

enjoying his golden years with his spouse in South Carolina. MSG [Ret.] Lambert was the witness to BG Edelman's hole-in-one.

About 10 months after Sept. 11, the New York Army National Guard soldiers completed the final clean-up at Ground Zero and came off 9/11 duty. They were ready for their next mission; some units were getting ready to deploy overseas. The next war, the Iraq war, began soon after the 9/11 terrorist attacks. The war started in 2003 and ended in 2011.

In 2004, the 42nd Infantry Division Headquarters – the headquarters that relieved the staff of the 53rd Troop Command two weeks after the attack – deployed to Iraq during the war.

Ron Sardanopoli

The Army National Guard continues to conduct its duties for domestic and foreign affairs with duty, honor and courage.

During a 53rd Troop Command headquarters 9/11 awards ceremony, I was an honoree amongst others. I was honored to receive the Meritorious Service Medal for meritorious service between Sept. 11 – Sept. 24, 2001. This is a New York State award signed by New York's Gov. George E. Pataki.

The award includes a citation that reads:

"Chief Sardanopoli distinguished himself while serving as the joint task force -1 [JTF-1] logistical officer during Operation Trade Center. While

Command and Control

serving as the G-4, Chief Sardanopoli's efforts were instrumental in the successful coordination of all logistical requirements in regards to the support/rescue mission at the World Trade Center.

Chief Sardanopoli performed in an outstanding manner under difficult and chaotic conditions. As a result of his distinguished management, the G-4 section logistically provided for the welfare of more than 4,100 activated soldiers. Furthermore, Chief Sardanopoli successfully coordinated the actions of assigned transportation and communications personnel to ensure that all activated soldiers were provided with necessary support services. His astute decision making and understanding of logistical requirements enabled the command to provide all requested support and services to those in need. Chief Sardanopoli's superior managerial and professional skills and outstanding dedication to duty reflects great credit upon himself, the 53rd Troop Command and the New York Army National Guard."

Command and Control

Chief Sardanopoli's Meritorious Service Medal for meritorious service for his service as a 1st responder during the 9-11 terrorist attack

Ron Sardanopoli

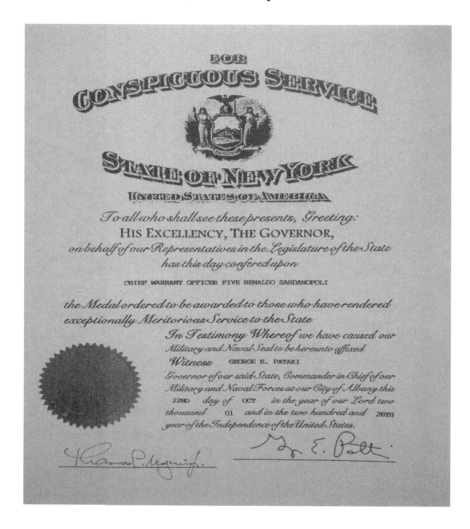

This certificate, signed by Gov. George E. Pataki, certifies that the Meritorious Service Medal is awarded to Chief Sardanopoli for exceptional Meritorious Service to the State of New York.

Command and Control

left to right, Maj. Gen. [Ret.] Stephen R. Seiter, Chief Warrant Officer -5 [Ret.] Ron Sardanopoli and Maj. Gen. [Ret.] Edward G. Klein. Photo taken at the 9-11, 53rd Troop Command awards ceremony event.

Ron Sardanopoli

I thanked our Commander, MG [R] Klein and Chief of Staff BG [R] Edelman for this award. I was honored to receive this award, but credit should go to my entire logistics team whose instincts went into gear.

My logistics team knew that their efforts were for a search and rescue mission to save lives and they all performed their duties with precision, honor and courage.

So did our logistics chain of command, starting with those unit supply sergeants who were located at Ground Zero. According to MG [R] Klein, our commander during 9/11, "The biggest compliments we received from the state and city officers of emergency management were for the Guard's ability to take over the management of all the supplies that were needed at Ground

Command and Control

Zero. Almost the entire Jacob Javits Center was full and there was no inventory or accountability. Within days the entire facility was emptied, inventoried and warehoused. As requests for supplies, tools and equipment came in, the Guard was able to deliver them where and when needed."

I also owe credit to those soldiers who represented our high source of supply, the director of logistics – DOL – and state maintenance officer – SMO – a staff member from each office was available to me at the 53rd Troop Command Emergency Operation Center to provide extra support and communications for quicker reactions to fill supply and maintenance needs.

Ron Sardanopoli

I also thank the 106th Rescue Wing, Col. [Ret.] Scuttina the Vice Wing Commander and his professional staff for supplementing our relatively small logistics staff that had to cover a 24-hour operation. They all deserve credit for this award.

My final thoughts as we approach the 20th anniversary of the 9/11 terrorist attack:

On July 1968, I bought into my oath that I would never fail my comrades and continue to believe in that same oath today. We have all seen things that leave their marks on us. We took these memories, dealt with them the best we can and try to lock them away somewhere in our mind. Sometimes soldiers fail and need help to deal with the demons and there is no shame in that. I hold my head up high and proud of who I am

Command and Control

today. To the 53rd Troop Command Army team and all of its subordinate units and soldiers, thank you for who you are and what you did. It has been my highest honor to serve alongside you. I feel humbled and blessed to be around to tell my story about the Sept. 11, 2001 World Trade Center attacks and the positive impact the New York Army National Guard's first responders and their replacement soldiers brought to the search and rescue mission.

The 53rd Troop Command and its actions during the deadliest attacks on American soil in U.S. history is an epic, yet gallant story.

The NYARNG 53rd Troop Command established a historical time in American history that should never be forgotten.

Ron Sardanopoli

About the Author

Command and Control

Ron Sardanopoli is grateful to have had the experience of serving in the New York Army National Guard for 36 years. He said, "It's 36 years and it is time to go."

When Ron took off his uniform for the last time and put on his jeans and sneakers, his thoughts of what tomorrow would bring lingered in his mind.

There had been offers to continue to work for the federal government in a civilian status, but those positions would have continued to keep him away from his family, and he had promised to give back his remaining time to the family.

Ron is humbled and honored to have served and has no regrets since leaving the military.

Ron Sardanopoli

He wants to see the Army National Guard embrace the communities and provide continued traditional support during disaster relief.

As this author reflects back from the first day of boot camp in 1968 to his retirement ceremony in 2004, he misses the heckling of comrade soldiers while strapping up in the locker room at the beginning of a duty day.

He misses the camaraderie and celebrations when the commander and staff met at a local restaurant for dinner and drinks, celebrating another successful mission.

Ron chooses to forget the pain he endured and the hard times he suffered. He chooses to leave the military with positive memories. Those memories include the realization of how strong he became, the lessons he learned and the pride in who he is as a result.

Ron retired with the satisfaction of knowing that his immediate family and his extended family are also proud of him.

Ron completed his graduate studies from the State University of New Paltz, New York with a master's degree in humanistic/multi-cultural education and provided motivational lectures to Blue Chip corporations and local businesses.

Blessed with a beautiful, fun, strong marriage, he thanks his wife Linda for putting up with him and for raising their children.

Those children, Renaldo and Danielle and grandchildren Valentino, Madison, Lucas, Leo and Mia know how much they're loved and that they come before anything.

Ron Sardanopoli

On a lighter note, Ron is excited that his daughter Danielle and son-in-law James's work remotely from home and along with the Sardanopoli's three grandchildren, now can live nearby.

The family is excited to be neighbors and to make new memories.

Ron's 36 years of military service opened a treasure chest of wonderful – and not so wonderful – experiences. There were journeys that went as planned and others that crashed on takeoff! He continues to use those military experiences as resources for his writing.

His stories are all fact-based about real people and real events. His hope is that after reading "Command and Control," Americans will realize the security and support that the Army National

Command and Control

Guard brings to our communities, homeland defense and overseas deployments.

Ron is a retired adjunct professor, a career Army chief warrant 5-CW5 commissioned officer and a retired veteran.

Ron is now the authors of non-fiction books, Amazon's five-star "Leap of Trust" and the recently-published "Command and Control" both are available on Amazon and at Barnes and Noble Booksellers.

His interest and focus are the riveting experiences that are surrounded with multi-cultural and inspirational people.

Ron continues to write at his home in Myrtle Beach, South Carolina. He and his wife Linda walk the beach each morning, catching the sunrise and taking in the ocean air. That jumpstarts his day in a blessed life.

From the Author

Sales of my previous book, "Leap of Trust," were gaining momentum in the early months of 2020 but because of the Covid-19 shutdowns, the early days of the pandemic hurt booksellers and publishers.

"Leap of Trust" is available at Barnes and Noble Booksellers which had been closed during the pandemic because of a government executive order requiring all book stores to close.

When the virus spread across the United States during the spring of 2020, most of the entertainment industry went into hibernation. Books remained available online but people were holding onto their funds in case of an economic catastrophic depression.

"Leap of Trust" never got the marketing opportunity that it deserved and sales almost came to a complete halt.

I tried my own marketing by telling Facebook friends about the book. Some of my Facebook friends purchased "Leap of Trust" online through Amazon, enjoyed the read and left five-star reviews.

Those Facebook friends increased from 200 to 5,000 which is the limit Facebook allows. If people wanted to "friend" me, they were only allowed to "follow" me so my followers also increased.

Some Facebook friends sent me their photos holding their copies of "Leap of Trust" to show their support of the book. Eventually I announced on Facebook that those who read "Leap of Trust" and would like their photo to be placed in my new release, "Command and Control" could privately message the picture to me.

For more information about "Leap of Trust, visit https://a.co/cvOTTU6.

Command and Control

I thank those Facebook friends for their support, and here are pictures of those who submitted them:

Ron Sardanopoli

Command and Control

Ron Sardanopoli

Command and Control

Ron Sardanopoli

Command and Control

Ron Sardanopoli

Command and Control

Ron Sardanopoli

The End

Made in the USA
Middletown, DE
02 November 2021